The Miraculous Journey of

EDWARD TULANE

The Miraculous Journey of
EDWARD TULANE

KATE DICAMILLO

WORKBOOK

Contents

뉴베리 상이란?

'아동 도서계의 노벨상!' 미국 최고 권위의 아동 문학상

뉴베리 상(Newbery Award)은 미국 도서관 협회에서 해마다 미국 아동 문학 발전에 가장 크게 이바지한 작가에게 수여하는 아동 문학상입니다. 1922년에 시작된이 상은 미국에서 가장 오랜 역사를 지닌 아동 문학상이자, '아동 도서계의 노벨상'이라 불릴 만큼 높은 권위를 자랑하는 상입니다.

뉴베리 상은 그 역사와 권위만큼이나 심사 기준이 까다롭기로 유명한데, 심사단은 책의 주제 의식은 물론 정보의 깊이와 스토리의 정교함, 캐릭터와 문체의 적정성 등을 꼼꼼히 평가하여 수상작을 결정합니다.

그해 최고의 작품으로 선정된 도서에게는 '뉴베리 메달(Newbery Medal)'이라고 부르는 금색 메달을 수여하며, 최종 후보에 올랐던 주목할 만한 작품들에게는 '뉴베리 아너(Newbery Honor)'라는 이름의 은색 마크를 수여합니다.

뉴베리 상을 받은 도서는 미국의 모든 도서관에 비치되어 더 많은 독자들을 만나게 되며, 대부분 수십에서 수백만 부가 판매되는 베스트셀러가 됩니다. 뉴베리상을 수상한 작가는 그만큼 필력과 작품성을 인정받게 되어, 수상 작가의 다른작품들 또한 수상작 못지않게 커다란 주목과 사랑을 받습니다.

왜 뉴베리 수상작인가?
쉬운 어휘로 쓰인 '검증된' 영어원서!

'뉴베리 수상작'들은 '검증된 원서'로 국내 영어 학습자들에게 큰 사랑을 받고 있습니다. '뉴베리 수상작'이 원서 읽기에 좋은 교재인 이유는 무엇일까요?

1. 아동 문학인 만큼 어휘가 어렵지 않습니다.
2. 어렵지 않은 어휘를 사용하면서도 '문학상'을 수상한 만큼 문장의 깊이가 상당합니다.
3. 적당한 난이도의 어휘와 깊이 있는 문장으로 구성되어 있기 때문에 초등 고학년부터 성인까지, 영어 초보자부터 실력자까지 모든 영어 학습자들이 읽기에 좋습니다.

실제로 뉴베리 수상작은 국제중·특목고에서는 입시 필독서로, 대학교에서는 영어 강독 교재로 다양하고 폭넓게 활용되고 있습니다. 이런 이유로 뉴베리 수상작은 한국어 번역서보다 오히려 원서가 훨씬 많이 판매되는 기현상을 보이고 있습니다.

'베스트 오브 베스트'만을 엄선한 「뉴베리 컬렉션」

「뉴베리 컬렉션」은 뉴베리 메달 및 아너 수상작, 그리고 뉴베리 수상 작가의 유명 작품들을 엄선하여 한국 영어 학습자들을 위한 최적의 교재로 재탄생시킨 영어 원서 시리즈입니다.

1. 어휘 수준과 문장의 난이도, 분량 등 국내 영어 학습자들에게 적합한 정도를 종합적으로 검토하여 선정하였습니다.
2. 기존 원서 독자층 사이의 인기도까지 감안하여 최적의 작품들을 선별하였습니다.
3. 판형이 좁고 글씨가 작아 읽기 힘들었던 원서 디자인을 대폭 수정하여, 판형을 시원하게 키우고 읽기에 최적화된 영문 서체를 사용하여 가독성을 극대화하였습니다.
4. 함께 제공되는 워크북은 어려운 어휘를 완벽하게 정리하고 이해력을 점검하는 퀴즈를 덧붙여 독자들이 원서를 보다 쉽고 재미있게 읽을 수 있도록 구성하였습니다.
5. 기존에 높은 가격에 판매되어 구입이 부담스러웠던 오디오북을 부록으로 제공하여 리스닝과 소리 내어 읽기에까지 원서를 두루 활용할 수 있도록 했습니다.

케이트 디카밀로(Kate DiCamillo)는 화려한 수상 경력을 가지고 있는, 미국의 대표적인 아동 문학 작가입니다. 그녀는 『Because of Winn-Dixie』로 뉴베리 아너를 수상하여 이름을 알리기 시작했고, 『The Tiger Rising』으로 전미도서상(National Book Award)의 최종 후보에 올랐습니다. 그리고 판타지 문학 작품인 『The Tale of Despereaux』는 "미국 아동 문학에 가장 크게 기여한" 작품이라는 평과 함께 뉴베리 메달을 수상하여 큰 인기몰이를 하였습니다. 또한 『The Miraculous Journey of Edward Tulane』으로 우수한 아동 문학에 수여하는 보스톤 글로브-혼 도서상(Boston Globe-Horn Book Award)을 받는 등 문학성을 여러 차례 검증 받고 있습니다.

『에드워드 툴레인의 신기한 여행(The Miraculous Journey of Edward Tulane)』은 도자기로 만들어진 토끼인형 에드워드(Edward)의 이야기를 담고 있습니다. 에드워드는 애빌린(Abilene)의 열살 생일 선물로, 할머니 펠레그리나(Pellegrina)가 주문해서 만든 인형입니다. 에드워드는 애빌린에게 많은 사랑을 받으며 살지만 가족들의 사랑과 배려에도 아무런 관심이 없습니다. 어느 날 밤, 애빌린은 이야기를 해달라고 했고 펠리그리나는 누구도 사랑하지 않아 흑멧돼지가 된 공주 이야기를 합니다. 그리고 펠리그리나는 에드워드에게 실망했다고 말합니다. 런던으로 가는 퀸 메리호에서 에드워드는 소년들의 장난에 의해 애빌린의 품을 떠나 바다로 내던져지게 됩니다. 이렇게 에드워드의 긴 여행이 시작됩니다.
이 책은 사랑 받을 줄만 알던 에드워드가 여행 중에 겪는 생생하고 다양한 사건들을 통해 성장해나가는 모습을 감동적으로 전하고 있습니다. 자신을 사랑해주던 소녀와 헤어지면서 비로소 에드워드는 진정한 사랑이 무엇인지 알게 됩니다. 뉴베리상 수상 작가인 케이트 디카밀로가 이 책을 통해 보내는 사랑의 메시지는 많은 사람들에게 감동을 줍니다.

이 책의 구성

원서 본문

내용이 담긴 원서 본문입니다.
원어민이 읽는 일반 원서와 같은 텍스트지만, 암기해야 할 중요 어휘들은 볼드체로 표시되어 있습니다. 이 어휘들은 지금 들고 계신 워크북에 챕터별로 정리되어 있습니다.

학습 심리학 연구 결과에 따르면, 한 단어씩 따로 외우는 단어 암기는 거의 효과가 없다고 합니다. 단어를 제대로 외우기 위해서는 문맥(context) 속에서 단어를 암기해야 하며, 한 단어당 문맥 속에서 15번 이상 마주칠 때 완벽하게 암기할 수 있다고 합니다.

이 책의 본문에서는 중요 어휘를 볼드체로 강조하여, 문맥 속의 단어들을 더 확실히 인지(word cognition in context)하도록 돕고 있습니다. 또한 대부분의 중요 단어들은 다른 챕터에서도 반복해서 등장하기 때문에 이 책을 읽는 것만으로도 자연스럽게 어휘력을 향상시킬 수 있습니다.

또한 본문 하단에는 내용 이해를 돕기 위한 '각주'가 첨가되어 있습니다. 각주는 굳이 암기할 필요는 없지만, 알아 두면 도움이 될 만한 정보를 설명하고 있습니다. 각주를 참고하면 스토리를 더 깊이 있게 이해할 수 있어 원서를 읽는 재미가 배가됩니다.

8

워크북(Workbook)

Check Your Reading Speed

해당 챕터의 단어 수가 기록되어 있어, 리딩 속도를 측정할 수 있습니다. 특히 리딩 속도를 중시하는 독자들이 유용하게 사용할 수 있습니다.

Build Your Vocabulary

본문에 볼드 표시되어 있던 단어들이 정리되어 있습니다. 리딩 전, 후에 반복해서 보면 원서를 더욱 쉽게 읽을 수 있고, 어휘력도 빠르게 향상될 것입니다.

단어는 〈스펠링 – 빈도 – 발음기호 – 품사 – 한글 뜻 – 영문 뜻〉 순서로 표기되어 있으며 빈도 표시(★)가 많을수록 필수 어휘입니다. 반복해서 등장하는 단어는 빈도 대신 '복습'으로 표기되어 있습니다. 품사는 아래와 같이 표기했습니다.

n. 명사 │ a. 형용사 │ ad. 부사 │ vi. 자동사 │ vt. 타동사 │ v. 자·타동사 모두 쓰이는 동사
conj. 접속사 │ prep. 전치사 │ int. 감탄사 │ phrasal v. 구동사 │ idiom 숙어 및 관용구

Comprehension Quiz

간단한 퀴즈를 통해 읽은 내용에 대한 이해력을 점검해 볼 수 있습니다.

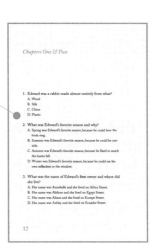

이 책의 활용법

「뉴베리 컬렉션」 이렇게 읽어 보세요!

아래와 같이 프리뷰(Preview) → 리딩(Reading) → 리뷰(Review) 세 단계를 거치면서 읽으면, 더욱 효과적으로 영어 실력을 향상할 수 있습니다!

1. 프리뷰(Preview) : 오늘 읽을 내용을 먼저 점검하자!

- 워크북을 통해 오늘 읽을 챕터에 나와 있는 단어들을 쭉 훑어봅니다. 어떤 단어들이 나오는지, 내가 아는 단어와 모르는 단어가 어떤 것들이 있는지 가벼운 마음으로 살펴봅니다.

- 평소처럼 하나하나 쓰면서 암기하려고 하지는 마세요! 익숙하지 않은 단어들을 주의 깊게 보되, 어차피 리딩을 하면서 점차 익숙해질 단어라는 것을 기억하며 빠르게 훑어봅니다.

- 뒤 챕터로 갈수록 '복습'이라고 표시된 단어들이 늘어나는 것을 알 수 있습니다. '복습' 단어인데도 여전히 익숙하지 않다면 더욱 신경을 써서 봐야겠죠? 매일매일 꾸준히 읽는다면, 익숙한 단어들이 점점 많아진다는 것을 몸으로 느낄 수 있습니다.

2. 리딩(Reading) : 내용에 집중하며 빠르게 읽어 나가자!

- 프리뷰를 마친 후 바로 리딩을 시작합니다. 방금 살펴봤던 어휘들을 문장 속에서 다시 만나게 되는데 이 과정에서 단어의 쓰임새와 어감을 자연스럽게 익히게 됩니다.

- 모르는 단어나 이해되지 않는 문장이 나오더라도 멈추지 말고 전체적인 맥락을 잡아가면서 속도감 있게 읽어 나가세요. 이해되지 않는 문장들은 따로 표시를 하되, 일단 넘어가고 계속 읽는 것이 좋습니다. 뒷부분을 읽다 보면 자연히 이해가 되는 경우도 있고, 정 이해가 되지 않는 부분은 리딩을 마친 이후에 따로 리뷰하는 시간을 가지면 됩니다. 문제집을 풀듯이 모든 문장을 분석하면서 원서를 읽는 것이 아니라, 리딩을 할 때는 리딩에만, 리뷰를 할 때는 리뷰에만 집중하는 것이 필요합니다.

- 볼드 처리된 단어의 의미가 궁금하더라도 워크북을 바로 펼치지 마세요. 정 궁금하다면 한 번씩 참고하는 것도 나쁘진 않지만, 워크북과 원서를 번갈아 보면서 읽는 것은 리딩의 흐름을 끊고 단어 하나하나에 집착하는 좋지 않은 리딩 습관을 심어 줄 수 있습니다.

- 같은 맥락에서 번역서를 구해 원서와 동시에 번갈아 보는 것도 좋은 방법이 아닙니다. 한글 번역을 가지고 있다고 해도 일단 영어로 읽을 때는 영어에만 집중하고 어느 정도 분량을 읽은 후에 번역서와 비교하도록 하세요. 모든 문장을

일일이 번역해서 완벽하게 이해하려는 것은 오히려 좋지 않은 리딩 습관을 심어 주어 장기적으로는 바람직하지 않은 결과를 얻을 수 있습니다. 처음부터 완벽하게 이해하려고 하는 것보다는 빠른 속도로 2~3회 반복해서 읽는 방식이 실력 향상에 더 도움이 됩니다. 만일 반복해서 읽어도 내용이 전혀 이해되지 않아 곤란하다면 책 선정에 문제가 있다고 할 수 있습니다. 그럴 때는 좀 더 쉬운 책을 골라 실력을 다진 뒤 다시 도전하는 것이 좋습니다.

- 초보자라면 분당 150단어의 리딩 속도를 목표로 잡고 리딩을 합니다. 분당 150단어는 원어민이 말하는 속도로, 영어 학습자들이 리스닝과 스피킹으로 넘어가기 위해 가장 기초적으로 달성해야 하는 단계입니다. 분당 50~80단어 정도의 낮은 리딩 속도를 가지고 있는 경우는 대부분 영어 실력이 부족해서라기보다 '잘못된 리딩 습관'을 가지고 있어서 그렇습니다. 이해력이 조금 떨어진다고 하더라도 분당 150단어까지는 속도에 대한 긴장감을 놓치지 말고 속도감 있게 읽어 나가도록 하세요.

3. 리뷰(Review) : 이해력을 점검하고 꼼꼼하게 다시 살펴보자!

- 해당 챕터의 Comprehension Quiz를 통해 이해력을 점검해 봅니다.
- 오늘 만난 어휘들을 다시 한번 복습합니다. 이때는 읽으면서 중요하다고 생각했던 단어를 연습장에 써 보면서 꼼꼼하게 외우는 것도 좋습니다.
- 이해가 되지 않는다고 표시해 두었던 부분도 주의 깊게 분석해 봅니다. 다시 한번 문장을 꼼꼼히 읽고, 어떤 이유에서 이해가 되지 않았는지 생각해 봅니다. 따로 메모를 남기거나 노트를 작성하는 것도 좋은 방법입니다.
- 사실 꼼꼼히 리뷰하는 것은 매우 고된 과정입니다. 원서를 읽고 리뷰하는 시간을 가지는 것이 영어 실력 향상에 많은 도움이 되기는 하지만, 이 과정을 철저히 지키려다가 원서 읽기의 재미를 반감시키는 것은 바람직하지 않습니다. 그럴 때는 차라리 리뷰를 가볍게 하는 것이 좋을 수 있습니다. '내용에 빠져서 재미있게', 문제집에서는 상상도 못할 '많은 양'을 읽으면서, 매일매일 조금씩 꾸준히 실력을 키워가는 것이 원서를 활용하는 기본적인 방법이며, 영어 공부의 왕도입니다. 문제집 풀듯이 원서 읽기를 시도하고 접근해서는 실패할 수밖에 없습니다.
- 이런 방식으로 원서를 끝까지 다 읽었다면, 다시 반복해서 읽거나 오디오북을 활용하는 등 다양한 방식으로 원서 읽기를 확장해 나갈 수 있습니다. 이에 대한 자세한 안내가 워크북 말미에 실려 있습니다.

1. Edward was a rabbit made almost entirely from what?
   A. Wood
   B. Silk
   C. China
   D. Plastic

2. What was Edward's favorite season and why?
   A. Spring was Edward's favorite season, because he could hear the birds sing.
   B. Summer was Edward's favorite season, because he could be outside.
   C. Autumn was Edward's favorite season, because he liked to watch the leaves fall.
   D. Winter was Edward's favorite season, because he could see his own reflection in the window.

3. What was the name of Edward's first owner and where did she live?
   A. Her name was Annabelle and she lived on Africa Street.
   B. Her name was Abilene and she lived on Egypt Street.
   C. Her name was Alison and she lived on Europe Street.
   D. Her name was Ashley and she lived on Ecuador Street.

4. How was Pelligrina responsible for Edward?
   A. She commissioned him and gave him as a present to Abilene.
   B. She made him new clothes when he needed them.
   C. She made sure that Abilene didn't take him to school.
   D. She made sure that the family dog didn't bite him.

5. How did Edward use the watch?
   A. It was gold and he hoped to sell it later.
   B. He used it as a chain to climb down from the table.
   C. It reflected his face well and he used it as a mirror.
   D. It was wound up by Abilene and showed him when she would come back.

6. From Edward's perspective, what was most damaged when the neighbor's dog, Rosie, came into their house?
   A. His china head
   B. His silk suit
   C. His ego
   D. The tablecloth

7. What emotion did Edward feel after Abilene found him again?
   A. He felt annoyed that the maid had treated him like an object.
   B. He felt anger that Abilene took so much time finding him.
   C. He felt upset because the other dolls teased him.
   D. He felt love that Abilene missed him.

1분에 몇 단어를 읽는지 리딩 속도를 측정해보세요.

$$\frac{1{,}027 \text{ words}}{\text{reading time (\quad) sec}} \times 60 = (\quad) \text{ WPM}$$

Build Your Vocabulary

entire*
[intáiər]

a. 전체의; 완전한 (entirely ad. 완전히)
You use entire when you want to emphasize that you are referring to the whole of something, for example, the whole of a place, time, or population.

paw*
[pɔ:]

n. (갈고리 발톱이 있는 동물의) 발; v. 앞발로 차다
The paws of an animal such as a cat, dog, or bear are its feet, which have claws for gripping things and soft pads for walking on.

torso
[tɔ́:rsou]

n. (인체의) 몸통; 토르소(머리·손발이 없는 나체 조각상)
Your torso is the main part of your body, and does not include your head, arms, and legs.

joint**
[dʒɔint]

v. ~을 접합하다; n. 관절; 연결 부위 (jointed a. 관절[마디]로 된)
Something that is jointed has joints that move.

wire**
[waiər]

n. 철사; 전선, 케이블; v. 철사로 매다; 전송하다, 전보로 알리다
A wire is a long thin piece of metal that is used to fasten things or to carry electric current.

bendable
[béndəbl]

a. 구부릴 수 있는; 융통성이 있는
A bendable object or material is capable of being bent or twisted without breaking.

arrange**
[əréindʒ]

v. 가지런히 하다, 배열하다; 준비하다
If you arrange things somewhere, you place them in a particular position, usually in order to make them look attractive or tidy.

reflect**
[riflékt]

v. 반영하다, 나타내다; 비추다, 반사하다
If something reflects an attitude or situation, it shows that the attitude or situation exists or it shows what it is like.

jaunty
[dʒɔ́:nti]

a. 쾌활한, 의기양양한, 경쾌한
If you describe someone or something as jaunty, you mean that they are full of confidence and energy.

ennui
[a:nwí:]

n. 권태감, 지루함
Ennui is a feeling of being tired, bored, and dissatisfied.

fluffy
[flʌ́fi]

a. 푹신한, 보풀의; 솜털의
If you describe something such as a towel or a toy animal as fluffy, you mean that it is very soft.

measure**
[méʒər]
vt. (~의) 길이[높이, 넓이]가 되다; 재다, 계량하다; n. 치수, 분량; (pl.) 수단, 방책
If something measures a particular length, width, or amount, that is its size or intensity, expressed in numbers.

tip*
[tip]
① n. (뾰족한) 끝 ② v. 뒤집어엎다, 기울이다 ③ n. 팁, 사례금
The tip of something long and narrow is the end of it.

penetrating
[pénətrèitiŋ]
a. 통찰력 있는, 예리한; (빛·소리·탄환 등이) 꿰뚫는, 관통하는
Someone who has a penetrating mind understands and recognizes things quickly and thoroughly.

intelligent**
[intélədʒənt]
a. 총명한, 똑똑한; 지능이 있는
A person or animal that is intelligent has the ability to think, understand, and learn things quickly and well.

exception**
[iksépʃən]
n. 예외, 이례, 특례; 제외 (exceptional a. 예외적인; 아주 뛰어난)
An exception is a particular thing, person, or situation that is not included in a general statement, judgment, or rule.

specimen*
[spésəmən]
n. 견본, 표본, 실례
A specimen of something is an example of it which gives an idea of what the whole of it is like.

whisker*
[wískər]
n. (고양이·쥐 등의) 수염; 구레나룻
The whiskers of an animal such as a cat or a mouse are the long stiff hairs that grow near its mouth.

pause**
[pɔːz]
n. 멈춤, 중지; vi. 중단하다, 잠시 멈추다
A pause is a short period when you stop doing something before continuing.

elegant**
[éligənt]
a. 품위 있는, 우아한, 고상한
If you describe a person or thing as elegant, you mean that they are pleasing and graceful in appearance or style.

origin**
[ɔ́ːridʒin]
n. 기원, 발단; 태생
You can refer to the beginning, cause, or source of something as its origin or origins.

initial**
[iníʃəl]
a. 처음의, 최초의; n. 이니셜, 머리글자 (initially a. 처음에, 시초에)
You use initial to describe something that happens at the beginning of a process.

unsavory
[ʌnséivəri]
a. 불쾌한, 고약한 냄새가 나는, 맛없는
If you describe a person, place, or thing as unsavory, you mean that you find them unpleasant or morally unacceptable.

bear**
[bɛər]
① v. 견디다; (의무·책임을) 지다; 낳다 ② n. 곰
If you bear an unpleasant experience, you accept it because you are unable to do anything about it.

consider***
[kənsídər]
v. 고려하다, 숙고하다
If you consider something, you think about it carefully.

prefer**
[prifə́ːr]
vt. ~을 좋아하다, 차라리 ~을 택하다
If you prefer someone or something, you like that person or thing better than another, and so you are more likely to choose them if there is a choice.

mistress *
[místris]

n. 여주인, 안주인
A dog's mistress is the woman or girl who owns it.

possession **
[pəzéʃən]

n. 소유, 소지, 보유
If you are in possession of something, you have it, because you have obtained it or because it belongs to you.

extraordinary *
[ikstrɔ́:rdənèri]

a. 기이한, 놀라운; 비상한, 비범한
If you describe something as extraordinary, you mean that it is very unusual or surprising.

wardrobe *
[wɔ́:rdròub]

n. 옷장; 의상
A wardrobe is a tall cupboard or cabinet in which you can hang your clothes.

compose *
[kəmpóuz]

vt. 구성하다, 조립하다; (마음을) 가라앉히다, 가다듬다
The things that something is composed of are its parts or members.

handmade
[hǽndméid]

a. 손으로 만든
Handmade objects have been made by someone using their hands or using tools rather than by machines.

custom ***
[kʌ́stəm]

a. (= custom-made) 주문한, 맞춤의; n. 풍습, 관습
Custom products or services are specially designed and made for a particular person.

fashion **
[fǽʃən]

vt. 만들어내다, 형성하다; n. 유행
If you fashion an object or a work of art, you make it.

specific **
[spisífik]

a. 명확한, 구체적인, 특정의 (specifically ad. 명확하게, 특히)
You use specific to refer to a particular fixed area, problem, or subject.

array *
[əréi]

n. 모음, 무리; 배열, 정렬; vt. 정렬시키다, 배열하다
An array of different things or people is a large number or wide range of them.

equip *
[ikwíp]

vt. 갖추다, 장비하다
If you equip a person or thing with something, you give them the tools or equipment that are needed.

fit ***
[fit]

① a. 알맞은, 적합한; v. 꼭 맞다, 어울리다 ② n. 발작, 경련
If something fits, it is the right size and shape to go onto a person's body or onto a particular object.

expressive
[iksprésiv]

a. 표정이 풍부한, 표정에 넘치는; 의미심장한; (감정 등을) 나타내는, 표현하는
If you describe a person or their behavior as expressive, you mean that their behavior clearly indicates their feelings or intentions.

wind ***
[waind]

① v. (wound-wound) 감다, 돌리다; n. 한 번 돌리기, 한 번 감음 ② n. 바람
When you wind something flexible around something else, you wrap it around it several times.

dining room *
[dáiniŋ rù:m]

n. 식당(방)
The dining room is the room in a house where people have their meals, or a room in a hotel where meals are served.

position[*][*]
[pəzíʃən]

vt. (특정한 장소에) 두다; n. 위치, 자세; 입장, 처지
If you position something somewhere, you put it there carefully, so that it is in the right place or position.

lead[*][*][*]
[li:d]

① vt. (led–led) 인도하다, 이끌다, 인솔하다; n. 선도, 솔선, 지휘 ② n. [광물] 납
If a road, gate, or door leads somewhere, you can get there by following the road or going through the gate or door.

stare[*]
[stɛər]

v. 응시하다, 뚫어지게 보다
If you stare at someone or something, you look at them for a long time.

tick
[tik]

n. (시계가) 똑딱이는 소리; v. (시계 따위가) 똑딱거리다
The tick of a clock or watch is the series of short sounds it makes when it is working, or one of those sounds.

reflection[*]
[riflékʃən]

n. (거울·물 등에 비친) 영상; 반사, 반영
A reflection is an image that you can see in a mirror or in glass or water.

cut a figure

idiom 어떤 인상을 주다; (남을) 매혹하다, (남의) 마음을 끌다
If you cut a fine figure, you have a fine appearance.

cease[*]
[si:s]

v. 그만두다, 중지하다
If you cease something, you stop it happening or working.

barely[*]
[bɛ́ərli]

ad. 간신히, 가까스로; 거의 ~없게
You use barely to say that something is only just true or only just the case.

tabletop
[téibltàp]

a. 테이블 윗면
A table top is the flat surface on a table.

duration[*]
[djuréiʃən]

n. 지속 시간[기간]; (시간의) 지속
The duration of an event or state is the time during which it happens or exists.

blind[*][*]
[blaind]

vt. 눈멀게 하다; a. 눈먼, 장님인 (blinding a. 눈이 부신; 눈을 뜰 수 없을 정도인)
If something blinds you, it makes you unable to see, either for a short time or permanently.

tablecloth[*]
[téiblklɔ̀:θ]

n. 식탁보, 테이블보
A tablecloth is a cloth used to cover a table.

charming[*]
[tʃɑ́:rmiŋ]

a. 매력 있는, 매력적인; 마법을 거는
If you say that something is charming, you mean that it is very pleasant or attractive.

request[*][*]
[rikwést]

vt. 바라다, 신청하다; n. 부탁, 요구
If you request something, you ask for it politely or formally.

phrase[*][*]
[freiz]

n. 구절, 관용구
A phrase is a short group of words that people often use as a way of saying something.

benefit[*]
[bénifit]

n. 혜택, 이득; v. 이익을 얻다, 득을 보다 (for the benefit of idiom ~을 위해)
If you say that someone is doing something for the benefit of a particular person, you mean that they are doing it for that person.

pretend***
[priténd]
v. 가장하다, ~인 체하다; a. 가짜의
If you pretend that something is the case, you act in a way that is intended to make people believe that it is the case, although in fact it is not.

courtesy*
[kə́ːrtisi]
n. 호의; 정중, 친절
If you refer to the courtesy of doing something, you are referring to a polite action.

condescend
[kàndəsénd]
vi. (우월감을 가지고) 베푸는 듯이 대하다; 자기를 낮추다, 겸손하게 굴다
(condescending a. 일부러 공손한, 생색 내는 듯한)
If you say that someone condescends to other people, you are showing your disapproval of the fact that they behave in a way which shows that they think they are superior to other people.

shine***
[ʃain]
v. (shone-shone) 빛나(게 하)다, 반짝이다; n. 빛, 빛남, 광채
Something that shines is very bright and clear because it is reflecting light.

responsible**
[rispánsəbl]
a. 책임이 있는; 믿을 만한
If someone or something is responsible for a particular event or situation, they are the cause of it or they can be blamed for it.

existence**
[igzístəns]
n. 존재, 실재, 현존
The existence of something is the fact that it is present in the world as a real thing.

commission*
[kəmíʃən]
v. (~하도록) 주문[의뢰, 위탁]하다; ~을 위임하다; n. 주문, 위탁; 위임, 임명
If you commission something or commission someone to do something, you formally arrange for someone to do a piece of work for you.

craftsman
[krǽftsmən]
n. 장인, 공예가
A craftsman is a man who makes things skillfully with his hands.

tuck*
[tʌk]
v. 밀어 넣다, 쑤셔 넣다; n. 접어 넣은 단
If you tuck something somewhere, you put it there so that it is safe, comfortable, or neat.

lie***
[lai]
vi. (lay-lain) 눕다, 누워 있다; 놓여 있다, 위치하다
If you are lying somewhere, you are in a horizontal position and are not standing or sitting.

in return
idiom 대답으로서, (~의) 대신으로
If you do something in return, you are doing it as a response or reaction.

crack**
[kræk]
n. 갈라진 금; 갑작스런 날카로운 소리; v. 금이 가다, 깨(지)다; 날카로운 소리를 내다
A crack is a very narrow gap between two things, or between two parts of a thing.

pinprick
[pínprik]
n. 바늘로 콕 찌름; 성가신 일; vt. 콕콕 찌르다
A pinprick is a prick caused by a pin.

comfort**
[kʌ́mfərt]
vt. 위로[위안]하다; n. 위로, 위안; 마음이 편안함, 안락
If you comfort someone, you make them feel less worried, unhappy, or upset, for example by saying kind things to them.

give way
idiom (〜에게) 양보하다
If one thing gives way to another, the first thing is replaced by the second.

dawn[*]
[dɔːn]
n. 새벽, 동틀 녘; vi. 날이 새다, 밝아지다; 나타나기 시작하다
Dawn is the time of day when light first appears in the sky, just before the sun rises.

Check Your Reading Speed

1분에 몇 단어를 읽는지 리딩 속도를 측정해보세요.

$$\frac{687 \text{ words}}{\text{reading time (} \quad \text{) sec}} \times 60 = (\quad) \text{ WPM}$$

Build Your Vocabulary

remarkable[*]
[rimá:rkəbl]

a. 주목할 만한; 비범한, 뛰어난
Someone or something that is remarkable is unusual or special in a way that makes people notice them and be surprised or impressed.

occasional[*]
[əkéiʒənl]

a. 가끔의, 때때로의
Occasional means happening sometimes, but not regularly or often.

domestic[*]
[dəméstik]

a. 가정의, 가정적인; 국내의, 자국의
A domestic situation or atmosphere is one which involves a family and their home.

brindled
[bríndld]

a. 줄무늬[반점]이 있는, 얼룩진
A brindled animal has brown or grey streaked or patched with a darker color.

inexplicable
[iniksplíkəbl]

a. 불가해한, 설명할 수 없는 (inexplicably ad. 설명할 수 없는 일이지만)
If something is inexplicable, you cannot explain why it happens or why it is true.

announce[***]
[ənáuns]

vt. 알리다, 공고하다, 전하다 (unannounced a. 예고 없는)
If you announce a piece of news or an intention, especially something that people may not like, you say it loudly and clearly, so that everyone you are with can hear it.

dining room[복습]
[dáiniŋ rùːm]

n. 식당(방)
The dining room is the room in a house where people have their meals, or a room in a hotel where meals are served.

tablecloth[복습]
[téiblklɔ̀ːθ]

n. 식탁보, 테이블보
A tablecloth is a cloth used to cover a table.

urine
[júərin]

n. 소변, 오줌
Urine is the liquid that you get rid of from your body when you go to the toilet.

trot[*]
[trat]

v. 빠른 걸음으로 가다; 총총걸음 치다; n. 빠른 걸음
When an animal such as a horse trots, it moves fairly fast, taking quick small steps.

sniff[**]
[snif]

v. 냄새를 맡다, 킁킁거리다; 콧방귀를 뀌다; n. 냄새 맡음; 콧방귀
If you sniff something or sniff at it, you smell it by sniffing.

consider[복습]
[kənsídər]

v. 고려하다, 숙고하다
If you consider something, you think about it carefully.

20

implication*
[ìmplikéiʃən]

n. 함축, 암시
Implication is a meaning that is not expressly stated but can be inferred.

vigorous*
[vígərəs]

a. 활발한, 원기 왕성한 (vigorously ad. 힘차게, 활기차게)
Vigorous physical activities involve using a lot of energy, usually to do short and repeated actions.

growl*
[graul]

v. 으르렁거리다; n. 으르렁거리는 소리
When a dog or other animal growls, it makes a low noise in its throat, usually because it is angry.

drool
[dru:l]

v. 군침을 흘리다, 침이 나오다; n. 군침
If a person or animal drools, saliva drops slowly from their mouth.

fortunately*
[fɔ́:rʃənətli]

ad. 다행히도, 운좋게도
Fortunately is used to introduce or indicate a statement about an event or situation that is good.

witness**
[wítnis]

v. 목격하다; 증언하다; n. 목격자, 증인
If you witness something, you see it happen.

suffer***
[sʌ́fər]

vi. 시달리다, 고통받다; 겪다, 당하다
If you suffer pain, you feel it in your body or in your mind.

obedience*
[oubí:diəns]

n. 복종, 순종, 준수
Obedience is the action that you do what you are told to do.

stain*
[stein]

v. 더러워지다, 얼룩지게 하다; n. 얼룩, 오점
If a liquid stains something, the thing becomes colored or marked by the liquid.

ache*
[eik]

vi. 쑤시다, 아프다; n. 아픔, 쑤심
If you ache or a part of your body aches, you feel a steady, fairly strong pain.

ego
[í:gou]

n. 자존심, 지나친 자부심; 자아
Someone's ego is their sense of their own worth. For example, if someone has a large ego, they think they are very important and valuable.

refer**
[rifə́:r]

v. 언급하다, 나타내다
If you refer to a particular subject or person, you talk about them or mention them.

outrage*
[áutreidʒ]

v. 격분[격노]하게 만들다; n. 격분, 격노
If you are outraged by something, it makes you extremely shocked and angry.

indignity
[indígnəti]

n. 모욕, 경멸, 냉대
If you talk about the indignity of doing something, you mean that it makes you feel embarrassed or unimportant.

jaw**
[dʒɔ:]

n. 턱, 아래턱
Your jaw is the lower part of your face below your mouth.

household[**] [háshòuld]

n. (한 집에 사는 사람들을 일컫는) 가정
A household is all the people in a family or group who live together in a house.

maid[*] [meid]

n. 하녀, 가정부; 소녀, 아가씨
A maid is a woman who works as a servant in a hotel or private house.

eager[***] [íːgər]

a. 열망하는, 간절히 하고 싶어 하는
If you are eager to do or have something, you want to do or have it very much.

impress[*] [imprés]

v. 깊은 인상을 주다, 감명을 주다
If something impresses you, you feel great admiration for it.

employer[**] [implóiər]

n. 고용주, 주인
Your employer is the person or organization that you work for.

diligent[*] [dílədʒənt]

a. 근면한, 성실한 (diligence n. 근면, 성실)
Someone who is diligent works hard in a careful and thorough way.

derogatory [dirágətɔ̀ːri]

a. 경멸적인, 깔보는
If you make a derogatory remark or comment about someone or something, you express your low opinion of them.

extreme[**] [ikstríːm]

n. 극단, 극도; 곤경, 위기; a. 극단의, 극도의
You can use extremes to refer to situations or types of behavior that have opposite qualities to each other, especially when each situation or type of behavior has such a quality to the greatest degree possible.

reckon[*] [rékən]

vt. ~라고 생각하다; 세다, 계산하다
If you reckon that something is true, you think that it is true.

dust[*] [dʌst]

v. 먼지를 털다[닦다]; n. 먼지, 티끌
When you dust something such as furniture, you remove dust from it, usually using a cloth.

vacuum[*] [vǽkjuəm]

v. 진공청소기로 청소하다; n. 공허, 공백; 진공
If you vacuum something, you clean it using a vacuum cleaner.

suck[**] [sʌk]

v. 빨다, 흡수하다; 삼키다; n. 빨아들임
If something sucks a liquid, gas, or object in a particular direction, it draws it there with a powerful force.

paw[복습] [pɔː]

v. (~을) 함부로 다루다; 앞발로 차다; n. (동물 · 갈고리 발톱이 있는) 발
If one person paws another, they touch or stroke them in a way that the other person finds offensive.

beat[**] [biːt]

v. (beat-beaten) 치다, 두들기다; (심장이) 고동치다; (날개를) 퍼덕거리다; n. [음악] 박자, 고동
If you beat someone or something, you hit them very hard.

brutality [bruːtǽləti]

n. 잔인성, 무자비, 만행
Brutality is cruel and violent treatment or behavior.

efficiency
[ifíʃənsi]

n. 능률, 효력
Efficiency is the quality of being able to do a task successfully, without wasting time or energy.

zeal*
[zi:l]

n. 열심, 열중
Zeal is great enthusiasm, especially in connection with work, religion, or politics.

lap*
[læp]

① n. 무릎; (트랙의) 한 바퀴 ② v. (파도가) 찰싹거리다, (할짝할짝) 핥다
If you have something on your lap, it is on top of your legs and near to your body.

maw
[mɔ:]

n. 입, 목구멍; (동물의) 위
If you describe something as a maw, you mean that it is like a big open mouth which swallows everything near it.

distress*
[distrés]

vt. 괴롭히다, 고민케 하다; n. 고통, 가난, 곤궁 (distressing a. 괴로움을 주는)
If someone or something distresses you, they cause you to be upset or worried.

clank
[klæŋk]

n. 철커덕 (소리); v. 철커덕 하는 소리가 나다
When large metal objects clank, they make a noise because they are hitting together or hitting against something hard.

shove*
[ʃʌv]

v. 밀어넣다, 밀치다, 밀어내다; n. 밀치기
If you shove something somewhere, you push it there quickly and carelessly.

awkward*
[ɔ́:kwərd]

a. 어색한, 불편한, 곤란한
Someone who feels awkward behaves in a shy or embarrassed way.

inhuman
[inhjú:mən]

a. 비인간적인, 잔인한, 냉혹한, 인정머리 없는
If you describe treatment or an action as inhuman, you mean that it is extremely cruel.

angle*
[æŋgl]

n. 각도, 각
An angle is the difference in direction between two lines or surfaces.

twitter
[twítər]

v. 지저귀다, 지저귀듯 지껄이다; n. (새의) 지저귐; 흥분
If you say that someone is twittering about something, you mean that they are speaking about silly or unimportant things, usually rather fast or in a high-pitched voice.

giggle*
[gigl]

v. 낄낄 웃다; n. 낄낄 웃음
If someone giggles, they laugh in a childlike way, because they are amused, nervous, or embarrassed.

flock*
[flɔk]

n. 무리, 떼; vi. 무리 짓다, 모이다
A flock of birds, sheep, or goats is a group of them.

demented
[diméntid]

a. 미친 듯이 구는
If you describe someone as demented, you think that their actions are strange, foolish, or uncontrolled.

leap*
[li:p]

v. 껑충 뛰다; 뛰어넘다; n. 뜀, 도약
If you leap, you jump high in the air or jump a long distance.

agitation
[ædʒitéiʃən]

n. 불안, 동요
If someone is in a state of agitation, they are very worried or upset, and show this in their behavior, movements, or voice.

annoyance[*]
[ənɔ́iəns]

n. 성가심, 불쾌감; 괴로움, 곤혹
Annoyance is the feeling that you get when someone makes you feel fairly angry or impatient.

mighty[*]
[máiti]

a. 강력한, 힘센 (mightily ad. 매우, 대단히)
Mighty is used to describe something that is very large or powerful.

inconvenience[*]
[ìnkənvíːnjəns]

vt. ~에게 불편을 느끼게 하다, 폐를 끼치다; n. 불편, 불편한 것
If someone inconveniences you, they cause problems or difficulties for you.

cavalier
[kævəlíər]

a. 무신경한 (cavalierly ad. 무신경하게)
If you describe a person or their behavior as cavalier, you are criticizing them because you think that they do not consider other people's feelings or take account of the seriousness of a situation.

inanimate
[inǽnəmət]

a. 생명 없는; 생기 없는, 활기 없는
An inanimate object is one that has no life.

satisfaction[**]
[sætisfǽkʃən]

n. 만족, 만족을 주는 것
Satisfaction is the pleasure that you feel when you do something or get something that you wanted or needed to do or get.

affair[***]
[əféər]

n. 사건; 일거리, 사무
You can refer to an important or interesting event or situation as the affair.

dismiss[**]
[dismís]

v. 해고하다, 내쫓다, 해산하다; (생각 등을) 떨쳐버리다
When an employer dismisses an employee, the employer tells the employee that they are no longer needed to do the job that they have been doing.

immediately[**]
[imíːdiətli]

ad. 곧바로, 즉시
If something happens immediately, it happens without any delay.

locate[*]
[lóukeit]

vt. (물건의 위치 등을) 알아내다; (어떤 장소에) 정하다
If you locate something or someone, you find out where they are.

bowel[*]
[bauəl]

n. ~의 가장 깊은 곳, ~의 내부; 창자, 장
You can refer to the parts deep inside something such as the earth, a building, or a machine as the bowels of that thing.

dent
[dent]

vt. 손상시키다, 움푹 들어가게 하다
If you dent the surface of something, you make a hollow area in it by hitting or pressing it.

mock[*]
[mak]

vt. 흉내 내며 놀리다, 조롱하다; n. 조롱, 놀림감; a. 가짜의, 모의의
(mocking a. 조롱하는)
If someone mocks you, they show or pretend that they think you are foolish or inferior, for example by saying something funny about you, or by imitating your behavior.

24

bow[*]
[bau]

① v. 머리를 숙이다, 굽히다 ② n. 활; 곡선
When you bow, you move your head or the top half of your body forward and downward as a formal way of greeting them or showing respect.

timepiece
[táimpìːs]

n. 시계
A timepiece is a clock, watch, or other device that measures and shows time.

incident[**]
[ínsidənt]

n. 일어난 일, 작은 사건
An incident is something that happens, often something that is unpleasant.

serve[***]
[səːrv]

v. 식사 시중을 들다, (음식을) 제공하다; (사람·조직·국가 등을 위해) 일하다, 복무하다; n. (테니스 등의) 서브
When you serve food and drink, you give people food and drink.

mention[***]
[ménʃən]

vt. 말하다, 언급하다; n. 언급, 진술
If you mention something, you say something about it, usually briefly.

1. How did Edward usually act when the family was talking around the dinner table?
   A. He made a point of not listening to the conversation.
   B. He listened carefully to every word of conversation.
   C. He waited for his chance to say something to everyone.
   D. He only listened to what Abilene had to say.

2. What did Edward compare Pellegrina to when she looked at him?
   A. A crow
   B. A hawk
   C. A snake
   D. A cat

3. In Pellegrina's story, why did it make no difference that the princess was beautiful?
   A. She was very ill and was going to die.
   B. She was very rich and could buy anything she wanted.
   C. She loved no one and cared nothing for love.
   D. She was blind and could not see her own beauty.

4. What did the princess in the story do with the ring that the prince gave her?
   A. She gave it to the queen for protection.
   B. She gave it back to the prince.
   C. She took it from her finger and swallowed it.
   D. She took it from her finger and threw it away.

5. Why did the witch turn the princess into a warthog?
   A. The princess broke into her house.
   B. The witch wanted to cook her for dinner.
   C. The princess wanted to be a strong animal.
   D. The princess said that she loved no one.

6. What did Pellegrina whisper to Edward?
   A. She said she was disappointed in him.
   B. She said she was proud of him.
   C. She said she was hopeful for him.
   D. She said she was angry with Abilene.

7. How did Edward feel about the story?
   A. He thought it was hilarious.
   B. He thought it was pointless.
   C. He thought it had a happy ending.
   D. He thought that Abilene might have nightmares from it.

1분에 몇 단어를 읽는지 리딩 속도를 측정해보세요.

$$\frac{426 \text{ words}}{\text{reading time (\quad) sec}} \times 60 = (\qquad) \text{ WPM}$$

Build Your Vocabulary

excruciating
[ikskrúːʃièitiŋ]

a. 맹렬한, 극심한; 극심한 고통을 주는 (excruciatingly ad. 극심하게)
If you describe something as excruciating, you mean that it is very unpleasant to experience, for example because it is very boring or embarrassing.

dull**
[dʌl]

a. 단조롭고 지루한, 활기 없는; 무딘, 둔한
If you describe someone or something as dull, you mean they are not interesting or exciting.

unusual**
[ʌnjúːʒuəl]

a. 예외적인, 드문, 보통이 아닌
If something is unusual, it does not happen very often or you do not see it or hear it very often.

force***
[fɔːrs]

vt. 강요하다, 억지로 밀어 넣다; n. 힘, 폭력; 군사력, 병력
If someone forces you to do something, they make you do it even though you do not want to, for example by threatening you.

attention***
[əténʃən]

n. 주의, 관심; 배려
If you give someone or something your attention, you look at it, listen to it, or think about it carefully.

lap**
[læp]

① n. 무릎; (트랙의) 한 바퀴 ② v. (파도가) 찰싹거리다, (할짝할짝) 핥다
If you have something on your lap, it is on top of your legs and near to your body.

nonsense**
[nánsens]

n. 터무니없는[말도 안 되는] 생각[말], 허튼소리
If you say that something spoken or written is nonsense, you mean that you consider it to be untrue or silly.

jovial
[dʒóuviəl]

a. 쾌활한, 명랑한, 재미있는 (jovially ad. 쾌활하게, 명랑하게)
If you describe a person as jovial, you mean that they are happy and behave in a cheerful way.

protect***
[prətékt]

v. 보호하다, 막다, 지키다
To protect someone or something means to prevent them from being harmed or damaged.

vantage
[væntidʒ]

n. 전망이 좋은 지점; 유리한 위치[지점]; 유리함, 우월
Vantage is a state, position, or opportunity affording superiority or advantage.

spread***
[spred]

v. 퍼지다, 펴다, 펼치다; 뿌리다; n. 퍼짐, 폭, 넓이
If something spreads or is spread by people, it gradually reaches or affects a larger and larger area or more and more people.

glitter[**]
[glítər]
vi. 반짝반짝 빛나다, 반짝이다; n. 반짝이는 작은 장식; 반짝거림, 광채
If something glitters, light comes from or is reflected off different parts of it.

array[복습]
[əréi]
n. 모음, 무리; 배열, 정렬; vt. 정렬시키다, 배열하다
An array of different things or people is a large number or wide range of them.

silverware
[sílvərwèər]
n. 은그릇, 은으로 된 식기류
You can use silverware to refer to all the things in a house that are made of silver, especially the cutlery and dishes.

amuse[**]
[əmjúːz]
vt. 즐겁게 하다, 재미나게 하다 (amused a. 즐거워[흥겨워]하는)
If something amuses you, it makes you want to laugh or smile.

condescend[복습]
[kàndəsénd]
vi. (우월감을 가지고) 베푸는 듯이 대하다; 자기를 낮추다, 겸손하게 굴다
(condescending a. 일부러 공손한, 생색 내는 듯한)
If you say that someone condescends to other people, you are showing your disapproval of the fact that they behave in a way which shows that they think they are superior to other people.

hawk[*]
[hɔːk]
n. [조류] 매
A hawk is a large bird with a short, hooked beak, sharp claws, and very good eyesight. Hawks catch and eat small birds and animals.

hang[***]
[hæŋ]
v. 배회하다; 매달리다; 달려 있다; 걸다, 달아매다; 교수형에 처하다
If something hangs in a high place or position, or if you hang it there, it is attached there so it does not touch the ground.

whisker[복습]
[wískər]
n. (고양이·쥐 등의) 수염; 구레나룻
The whiskers of an animal such as a cat or a mouse are the long stiff hairs that grow near its mouth.

dim[*]
[dim]
a. 어둑한, 흐릿한, 희미한; v. 어둑하게 하다, 흐려지다
If you have a dim memory or understanding of something, it is difficult to remember or is unclear in your mind.

shiver[*]
[ʃívəːr]
n. 떨림, 전율; v. (추위·공포로) 후들후들 떨다; 전율하다
A shiver is a shaking or trembling, as from fear or cold.

arrange[복습]
[əréindʒ]
v. 가지런히 하다, 배열하다; 준비하다
If you arrange things somewhere, you place them in a particular position, usually in order to make them look attractive or tidy.

cough[**]
[kɔːf]
v. 기침하다; n. 기침
When you cough, you force air out of your throat with a sudden, harsh noise. You often cough when you are ill, or when you are nervous or want to attract someone's attention.

1분에 몇 단어를 읽는지 리딩 속도를 측정해보세요.

$$\frac{937 \text{ words}}{\text{reading time (} \quad \text{) sec}} \times 60 = (\quad) \text{ WPM}$$

Build Your Vocabulary

shine ^{복습}
[ʃain]

v. (shone–shone) 빛나(게 하)다, 반짝이다; n. 빛, 빛남, 광채
Something that shines is very bright and clear because it is reflecting light.

moonless
[múːnlis]

a. (하늘에) 달이 없는
A moonless sky or night is dark because there is no moon.

stare ^{복습}
[stɛər]

v. 응시하다, 뚫어지게 보다
If you stare at someone or something, you look at them for a long time.

shiver ^{복습}
[ʃívəːr]

n. 떨림, 전율; v. (추위·공포로) 후들후들 떨다; 전율하다
A shiver is a shaking or trembling, as from fear or cold.

neighboring[*]
[néibəriŋ]

a. 근처에 있는[사는], 인근의
Neighboring places or things are near other things of the same kind.

immediately^{복습}
[imíːdiətli]

ad. 곧바로, 즉시
If something happens immediately, it happens without any delay.

swallow^{**}
[swálou]

v. 삼키다, 목구멍으로 넘기다; (초조해서) 마른침을 삼키다
If you swallow something, you cause it to go from your mouth down into your stomach.

wander[*]
[wándər]

v. 돌아다니다, 방황하다; n. 유랑, 방랑
If you wander in a place, you walk around there in a casual way, often without intending to go in any particular direction.

hut[*]
[hʌt]

n. (간단하게 집이나 쉼터로 지은) 오두막
A hut is a small house with only one or two rooms, especially one which is made of wood, mud, grass, or stones.

witch[*]
[witʃ]

n. 마녀
In fairy stories, a witch is a woman, usually an old woman, who has evil magic powers.

concern^{**}
[kənsə́ːrn]

n. 관심(사); 염려, 걱정; vt. 염려하다; ~에 관계하다; 관심을 갖다
Someone's concerns are the things that they consider to be important.

consequence[*]
[kánsikwəns]

n. 결과, 결말; 중요성, 중대함
The consequences of something are the results or effects of it.

dare[*]
[dɛər]

v. 감히 ~하다, 무릅쓰다, 도전하다
If you dare to do something, you do something which requires a lot of courage.

stamp[**]
[stæmp]

v. (발을) 구르다, 짓밟다; 날인하다; n. 우표, 인지; 도장
If you stamp or stamp your foot, you lift your foot and put it down very hard on the ground, for example because you are angry.

squeal
[skwiːl]

v. 꺅꺅거리다, 비명을 지르다; n. 꽥꽥거리는 소리
If someone or something squeals, they make a long, high-pitched sound.

slit[*]
[slit]

v. (slit-slit) ~을 잘라내다, ~을 가느다랗게 베다[째다]; n. 갈라진 틈, 틈새
If you slit something, you make a long narrow cut in it.

belly[*]
[béli]

n. 배, 복부
The belly of a person or animal is their stomach or abdomen.

feed[**]
[fiːd]

vt. (fed-fed) 먹이를 주다, 음식을 먹이다; 공급하다
If you feed a person or animal, you give them food to eat and sometimes actually put it in their mouths.

butcher[*]
[bútʃər]

vt. 도살하다, 학살하다; n. 고깃간 주인, 도살업자, 학살자
To butcher an animal means to kill it and cut it up for meat.

indignant[*]
[indígnənt]

a. 분개한, 화난 (indignantly ad. 분개하여, 화나서)
If you are indignant, you are shocked and angry, because you think that something is unjust or unfair.

nod[**]
[nad]

v. 끄덕이다, 끄덕여 표시하다; n. (동의·인사·신호·명령의) 끄덕임
If you nod, you move your head downward and upward to show agreement, understanding, or approval.

lean[**]
[liːn]

① v. 상체를 굽히다; 기대어 세우다, 기울다; 기대다, 의지하다 ② a. 야윈, 마른
When you lean in a particular direction, you bend your body in that direction.

whisper[*]
[hwíspəːr]

v. 속삭이다
When you whisper, you say something very quietly.

lie[복습]
[lai]

vi. (lay-lain) 눕다, 누워 있다; 놓여 있다, 위치하다
If you are lying somewhere, you are in a horizontal position and are not standing or sitting.

pointless
[pɔ́intlis]

a. 무의미한, 할 가치가 없는
If you say that something is pointless, you are criticizing it because it has no sense or purpose.

gruesome
[grúːsəm]

a. 소름 끼치는, 무시무시한; 힘든
Something that is gruesome is extremely unpleasant and shocking.

grotesque
[groutésk]

a. 괴상한, 그로테스크한, 기괴한
You say that something is grotesque when it is so unnatural, unpleasant, and exaggerated that it upsets or shocks you.

fate[*]
[feit]

n. 운명, 숙명
A person's or thing's fate is what happens to them.

agitate
[ǽdʒitèit]

v. 흔들다, 선동하다, 교란하다 (agitated a. 흥분한; 동요한)

If something agitates you, it worries you and makes you unable to think clearly or calmly.

description**
[diskrípʃən]

n. 서술, 기술, 묘사

A description of someone or something is an account which explains what they are or what they look like.

comfort^{복습}
[kʌ́mfərt]

n. 마음이 편안함, 안락; 위로, 위안; vt. 위로[위안]하다

If you are doing something in comfort, you are physically relaxed and contented, and are not feeling any pain or other unpleasant sensations.

dawn^{복습}
[dɔ:n]

n. 새벽, 동틀 녘; vi. 날이 새다, 밝아지다; 나타나기 시작하다

Dawn is the time of day when light first appears in the sky, just before the sun rises.

Chapters Five & Six

1. What was the Tulane family busy preparing for?
   A. They were preparing Edward for a new owner.
   B. They were preparing for a trip by train to Louisiana.
   C. They were preparing for a trip by ship to London.
   D. They were preparing to travel all around the world by ship.

2. How did people react to Edward aboard the ship?
   A. Most people thought Edward was a real rabbit.
   B. They paid a lot of attention to Edward.
   C. Most people simply ignored Edward, especially children.
   D. They wondered if rabbits could ride on ships.

3. Which of the following did the boys, Martin and Amos, NOT do with Edward?
   A. They asked if he did anything special, like wind-up.
   B. They removed his clothing.
   C. They bent his ears and arms backward.
   D. They tossed him back and forth.

4. What was even worse for Edward than being naked on the ship?
   A. Being thrown around while naked
   B. Being laughed at while naked
   C. Being cold and naked
   D. Being dropped on the floor while naked

5. What happened when Abilene tried to stop the boys from throwing Edward?
   A. They held Edward up above her head.
   B. They dropped Edward on the ship's deck.
   C. They accidentally threw Edward overboard.
   D. They put Edward's clothes back on him.

6. How did Edward feel when he saw Abilene holding his gold pocket watch?
   A. He thought that Abilene might lose it.
   B. He thought he needed his watch.
   C. He wanted Abilene to throw the watch to him.
   D. He loved Abilene and would miss her.

7. What was the first genuine emotion that Edward felt when he landed on the ocean floor?
   A. He was excited.
   B. He was cold.
   C. He was upset.
   D. He was afraid.

1분에 몇 단어를 읽는지 리딩 속도를 측정해보세요.

$$\frac{791 \text{ words}}{\text{reading time ( ) sec}} \times 60 = (\qquad) \text{ WPM}$$

Build Your Vocabulary

frantic[*]
[frǽntik]

a. 극도로 흥분한, 광란의
If you are frantic, you are behaving in a wild and uncontrolled way because you are frightened or worried.

voyage[*]
[vɔ́iidʒ]

n. 항해, 여행; v. 항해하다, 여행하다
A voyage is a long journey on a ship or in a spacecraft.

possess[***]
[pəzés]

vt. 소유하다, 가지고 있다
If you possess something, you have it or own it.

cut a figure[복습]

idiom 어떤 인상을 주다; (남을) 매혹하다, (남의) 마음을 끌다
If you cut a fine figure, you have a fine appearance.

outfit[**]
[áutfit]

n. 한 벌의 옷, 복장
An outfit is a set of clothes.

display[***]
[displéi]

v. 보이다, 나타내다, 진열[전시]하다; n. 전시, 진열품; 표시
If you display something, you show it to people.

derby
[dɔ́:rbi]

n. 중산모자
A derby is a felt hat that is round and hard with a narrow brim.

railing
[réiliŋ]

n. 가드레일, 난간
A fence made from metal bars is called a railing or railings.

dock[*]
[dak]

n. 선창, 부두; v. 부두에 들어가다; (우주선이) 도킹하다
A dock is an enclosed area in a harbor where ships go to be loaded, unloaded, and repaired.

floppy
[flápi]

a. 퍼덕퍼덕 펄럭이는; 늘어진, 느슨한
Something that is floppy is loose rather than stiff, and tends to hang downward.

string[***]
[striŋ]

v. (strung–strung) 묶다, 매달다; n. 끈, 실; (악기의) 현[줄]
If you string something somewhere, you hang it up between two or more objects.

glow[***]
[glou]

v. 빛을 내다, 빛나다; n. 빛, 밝음
If something glows, it produces a dull, steady light.

damp[**]
[dæmp]

a. 축축한; n. 습기
Something that is damp is slightly wet.

suppose***
[səpóuz]

v. (~이라고) 생각하다; 가정하다
If you suppose that something is true, you believe that it is probably true, because of other things that you know.

clutch**
[klʌtʃ]

v. 꽉 잡다, 붙들다, 부여잡다; n. 붙잡음, 움켜쥠
If you clutch at something or clutch something, you hold it tightly, usually because you are afraid or anxious.

fierce**
[fiərs]

a. 격렬한, 지독한; 사나운 (fiercely ad. 맹렬히, 사납게)
Fierce feelings or actions are very intense or enthusiastic, or involve great activity.

result***
[rizʌlt]

v. (결과로서) 생기다, 일어나다; n. 결과; 성과
If something results in a particular situation or event, it causes that situation or event to happen.

wrinkle*
[riŋkl]

v. 주름이 지다, 구겨지다; n. 주름, 잔주름
If cloth wrinkles, or if someone or something wrinkles it, it gets folds or lines in it.

relieve**
[rilíːv]

vt. (걱정·고통 등을) 덜다, 안도하게 하다, 완화하다
(relieved a. 안도하는, 다행으로 여기는)
If something relieves an unpleasant feeling or situation, it makes it less unpleasant or causes it to disappear completely.

exact**
[igzǽkt]

v. 받아 내다, 요구하다; (남에게 나쁜 일을) 가하다[일으키다]; a. 정확한, 정밀한
When someone exacts something, they demand and obtain it from another person, especially because they are in a superior or more powerful position.

attention*복습
[əténʃən]

n. 주의, 관심; 배려
If you give someone or something your attention, you look at it, listen to it, or think about it carefully.

singular*
[síŋgjulər]

a. 뛰어난, 보기 드문; 유일한, 단독의; 기묘한, 이상한
Singular means very great and remarkable.

glance*
[glæns]

n. 흘긋 봄; v. 흘긋 보다, 잠깐 보다
A glance is a quick look at someone or something.

longing**
[lɔ́ːŋiŋ]

n. 갈망, 열망; a. 갈망하는, 동경하는
If you feel longing or a longing for something, you have a rather sad feeling because you want it very much.

particular***
[pərtíkjələr]

a. 특정한, 특별한, 특유의
You use particular to emphasize that you are talking about one thing or one kind of thing rather than other similar ones.

deck***
[dek]

n. 갑판; (카드 패의) 한 벌
A deck on a vehicle such as a bus or ship is a lower or upper area of it.

wind*복습
[waind]

① v. 감다, 돌리다; n. 한 번 돌리기, 한 번 감음 ② n. 바람
When you wind up a mechanical device, for example a watch or a clock, you turn a knob, key, or handle on it several times in order to make it operate.

thoughtful*
[θɔ́:tfəl]

a. 생각에 잠긴; 사려 깊은, 신중한
If you are thoughtful, you are quiet and serious because you are thinking about something.

pause^{복습}
[pɔ:z]

n. 멈춤, 중지; vi. 중단하다, 잠시 멈추다
A pause is a short period when you stop doing something before continuing.

pajama
[pədʒá:mə]

n. (pl.) 파자마, 잠옷; a. 파자마 같은
A pair of pajamas consists of loose trousers and a loose jacket that people wear in bed.

disregard*
[dìsrigá:rd]

vt. 무시하다, 경시하다; n. 무시, 경시
If you disregard something, you ignore it or do not take account of it.

breeze*
[bri:z]

n. 산들바람; vi. 산들바람이 불다
A breeze is a gentle wind.

billow*
[bílou]

vi. (바람에) 부풀어 오르다; (연기·구름이) 피어오르다
When something made of cloth billows, it swells out and moves slowly in the wind.

straw^{**}
[strɔ:]

n. 짚, 밀짚; 빨대
Straw consists of the dried, yellowish stalks from crops such as wheat or barley.

boater
[bóutər]

n. 밀짚모자; 보트 타는 사람
A boater or a straw boater is a hard straw hat with a flat top and brim which is often worn for certain social occasions in the summer.

dashing*
[dǽʃiŋ]

a. 늠름한, 기세 좋은
A dashing person or thing is very stylish and attractive.

grab*
[græb]

v. 부여잡다, 움켜쥐다; n. 부여잡기
If you grab something, you take it or pick it up suddenly and roughly.

rip*
[rip]

v. 찢다, 벗겨내다; 돌진하다; n. 찢어진 틈, 잡아 찢음
When something rips or when you rip it, you tear it forcefully with your hands or with a tool such as a knife.

merrily
[mérəli]

ad. 즐겁게, 명랑하게
If you say that something is happening merrily, you mean that it is happening fairly quickly, and in a pleasant or satisfactory way.

underwear
[ʌ́ndərwɛər]

n. 속옷, 내의류
Underwear is clothing such as vests and pants which you wear next to your skin under your other clothes.

aloft*
[əlɔ́:ft]

ad. 위에, 높이, 공중에
Something that is aloft is in the air or off the ground.

mortify*
[mɔ́:rtəfài]

vt. 굴욕을 느끼게 하다, 분하게 하다
If you say that something mortifies you, you mean that it offends or embarrasses you a great deal.

naked^{**}
[néikid]

a. 나체의, 발가벗은; 적나라한
Someone who is naked is not wearing any clothes.

38

except[***]
[iksépt]

prep. ~를 제외하고, ~외에는 ; vt. ~을 빼다, 제외하다
You use except for to introduce the only thing or person that prevents a statement from being completely true.

passenger[***]
[pǽsəndʒər]

n. 승객
A passenger in a vehicle such as a bus, boat, or plane is a person who is traveling in it, but who is not driving it or working on it.

curious[***]
[kjúəriəs]

a. 궁금한, 호기심이 많은; 별난, 특이한
If you are curious about something, you are interested in it and want to know more about it.

embarrass[**]
[imbǽrəs]

v. 부끄럽게[무안하게] 하다; 당황하게 하다 (embarrassed a. 당혹한, 창피한)
If something or someone embarrasses you, they make you feel shy or ashamed.

clap[**]
[klæp]

v. 박수를 치다
When you clap, you hit your hands together to show appreciation or attract attention.

shipload
[ʃíplòud]

n. 다량, 다수; 배 한 척분의 적하량
A shipload of people or goods is as many people or goods as a ship can carry.

grubby
[grʌ́bi]

a. 더러운, 지저분한
A grubby person or object is rather dirty.

triumphant[*]
[traiʌ́mfənt]

a. 의기양양한; 크게 성공한 (triumphantly ad. 의기양양하게)
Someone who is triumphant has gained a victory or succeeded in something and feels very happy about it.

tackle[*]
[tækl]

v. 달려들다, 태클하다; n. 연장, 도구
If you tackle someone, you attack them and fight them.

shove[복습]
[ʃʌv]

v. 밀치다, 밀어넣다, 밀어내다; n. 밀치기
If you shove something somewhere, you push it there quickly and carelessly.

upset[**]
[ʌpsét]

v. (계획 등을) 망쳐놓다; 뒤엎다; 당황하게 하다
If events upset something such as a procedure or a state of affairs, they cause it to go wrong.

aim[***]
[eim]

n. 겨냥, 조준; 목적, 뜻; v. 겨냥을 하다, 목표삼다
Your aim is your skill or action in pointing a weapon or other object at its target.

overboard[*]
[óuverbɔːrd]

ad. 배 밖으로[에]
If you fall overboard, you fall over the side of a boat into the water.

1분에 몇 단어를 읽는지 리딩 속도를 측정해보세요.

$$\frac{327 \text{ words}}{\text{reading time (}\quad\text{) sec}} \times 60 = (\quad\quad) \text{ WPM}$$

Build Your Vocabulary

drown[**]
[draun]

v. 물에 빠지다, 익사하다; (물에) 빠뜨리다, 익사시키다
When someone drowns or is drowned, they die because they have gone or been pushed under water and cannot breathe.

ridiculous[**]
[ridíkjuləs]

a. 터무니없는, 웃기는, 우스꽝스러운
If you say that something or someone is ridiculous, you mean that they are very foolish.

tumble[**]
[tʌmbl]

v. 굴러 떨어지다, 넘어지다; n. 추락; 폭락
If someone or something tumbles somewhere, they fall there with a rolling or bouncing movement.

glimpse[***]
[glimps]

n. 흘끗 봄[보임]; v. 흘끗 보다
If you get a glimpse of someone or something, you see them very briefly and not very well.

railing[복습]
[réiliŋ]

n. 가드레일, 난간
A fence made from metal bars is called a railing or railings.

reflect[복습]
[riflékt]

v. 반사하다, 비추다; 반영하다, 나타내다
When light, heat or other rays reflect off a surface or when a surface reflects them, they are sent back from the surface and do not pass through it.

tremendous[**]
[triméndəs]

a. 거대한, 대단한; 엄청난, 무서운
You use tremendous to emphasize how strong a feeling or quality is, or how large an amount is.

force[복습]
[fɔːrs]

n. 힘, 폭력; 군사력, 병력; vt. 강요하다, 억지로 밀어 넣다
Force is the power or strength which something has.

sink[***]
[siŋk]

v. 가라앉다, 침몰하다
If something sinks, it disappears below the surface of a mass of water.

witness[복습]
[wítnis]

v. 목격하다; 증언하다; n. 목격자, 증인
If you witness something, you see it happen.

aboard[*]
[əbɔ́ːrd]

ad. 배에, 승선하여
If you are aboard a ship or plane, you are on it or in it.

blithe[*]
[blaið]

a. 태평스러운; 즐거운, 유쾌한, 쾌활한 (blithely ad. 태평스럽게; 쾌활하게)
You use blithe to indicate that something is done casually, without serious or careful thought.

muck
[mʌk]

n. 쓰레기, 오물; 거름, 퇴비; vt. 실패하다, 망쳐놓다
Muck is dirt or some other unpleasant substance.

genuine**
[dʒénjuin]

a. 진심의, 참된; 진짜의, 진품의
Genuine refers to things such as emotions that are real and not pretended.

Chapters Seven & Eight

1. What did Edward think would happen to him at the bottom of the ocean?
   A. He thought that Abilene would certainly come and find him.
   B. He thought that a shark might eat him.
   C. He thought that he might drown after a few days.
   D. He thought that he might float back up to the surface.

2. How did Edward feel about Pellegrina?
   A. He thought that she might know exactly where to find him.
   B. He wondered if she would go to London to visit Abilene.
   C. He hoped that she would make a new china rabbit for Abilene.
   D. He felt that she was somehow responsible for what happened to him.

3. How did Edward move from the ocean floor?
   A. A fish swam into him and he floated up.
   B. A storm lifted him from the ocean floor.
   C. Someone in a submarine saw him and took him away.
   D. A diver grabbed him from the ocean floor.

4. How did the fisherman react to Edward when he was found in his net?

   A. He wanted to throw him back in the ocean.

   B. He wanted to attach him to his ship.

   C. He wanted to take Edward home and try to fix him.

   D. He wanted to give it to the younger man as a gift for his daughter.

5. How did the fisherman carry Edward back home?

   A. He put Edward in a plastic bag.

   B. He carried Edward on one shoulder.

   C. He carried Edward by his ears.

   D. He held Edward in front of him with both hands.

6. What did the fisherman show Edward on the way back home?

   A. He showed Edward the North Star.

   B. He showed Edward his favorite restaurant.

   C. He showed Edward pictures of his wife and children.

   D. He showed Edward his old rabbit toy.

7. What did Nellie say that confused Edward?

   A. Nellie said that he was made of wood.

   B. Nellie asked if he was an American or a British rabbit.

   C. Nellie referred to him as a cat instead of a rabbit.

   D. Nellie referred to him as a girl instead of a boy.

1분에 몇 단어를 읽는지 리딩 속도를 측정해보세요.

$$\frac{772 \text{ words}}{\text{reading time ( ) sec}} \times 60 = (\quad) \text{ WPM}$$

Build Your Vocabulary

pretend
[priténd]

v. 가장하다, ~인 체하다; a. 가짜의
If you pretend that something is the case, you act in a way that is intended to make people believe that it is the case, although in fact it is not.

dining room
[dáiniŋ rùːm]

n. 식당(방)
The dining room is the room in a house where people have their meals, or a room in a hotel where meals are served.

wonder^{**}
[wʌ́ndər]

v. 이상하게 여기다, 호기심을 가지다; n. 경탄할 만한 것, 경이
If you wonder about something, you think about it because it interests you and you want to know more about it.

further[*]
[fə́ːrðər]

ad. (far–further–furthest) 더 멀리
Further means a greater distance than before or than something else.

consider
[kənsídər]

v. 고려하다, 숙고하다
If you consider something, you think about it carefully.

fate
[feit]

n. 운명, 숙명
A person's or thing's fate is what happens to them.

witch
[witʃ]

n. 마녀
In fairy stories, a witch is a woman, usually an old woman, who has evil magic powers.

responsible
[rispánsəbl]

a. 책임이 있는; 믿을 만한
If someone or something is responsible for a particular event or situation, they are the cause of it or they can be blamed for it.

overboard
[óuvərbɔ̀ːrd]

ad. 배 밖으로[에]
If you fall overboard, you fall over the side of a boat into the water.

punish^{**}
[pʌ́niʃ]

v. 벌하다, 응징하다, 처벌하다
To punish someone means to make them suffer in some way because they have done something wrong.

ordeal[*]
[ɔːrdíːəl]

n. 호된 시련, 고된 체험
If you describe an experience or situation as an ordeal, you think it is difficult and unpleasant.

lead ^{복습}
[li:d]

① vt. (led—led) 인도하다, 이끌다, 인솔하다; n. 선도, 솔선, 지휘 ② n. [광물] 납

If something leads to a situation or event, usually an unpleasant one, it begins a process which causes that situation or event to happen.

spin ^{**}
[spin]

v. 돌리다, 맴돌리다; 오래[질질] 끌다; n. 회전

If something spins or if you spin it, it turns quickly around a central point.

pummel
[pʌ́məl]

vt. (연달아) 주먹으로 치다, 연타하다

If you pummel someone or something, you hit them many times using your fists.

shove ^{복습}
[ʃʌv]

v. 밀치다, 밀어넣다, 밀어내다; n. 밀치기

If you shove something somewhere, you push it there quickly and carelessly.

ferocity [*]
[fərásəti]

n. 흉포함; 흉포한 행동

The ferocity of something is its fierce or violent nature.

fling ^{**}
[fliŋ]

vt. (flung—flung) 내던지다, 던지다; (문 등을) 왈칵 열다

If you fling something somewhere, you throw it there using a lot of force.

glimpse ^{복습}
[glimps]

v. 흘끗 보다; n. 흘끗 봄[보임]

If you glimpse someone or something, you see them very briefly and not very well.

bruise ^{**}
[bru:z]

v. 멍들게 하다, 타박상을 입히다; n. 타박상, 멍 (bruised a. 멍든)

If you bruise a part of your body, a bruise appears on it, for example because something hits you.

rush ^{**}
[rʌʃ]

v. 돌진하다, 급히 움직이다, 서두르다; n. 돌진; 쇄도

If air or liquid rushes somewhere, it flows there suddenly and quickly.

appreciate ^{**}
[əprí:ʃieit]

vt. 고맙게 생각하다; 평가하다, 감상하다

If you appreciate something that someone has done for you or is going to do for you, you are grateful for it.

depth ^{**}
[depθ]

n. 깊은 곳, 깊음; 깊이

The depths are places that are a long way below the surface of the sea or earth.

wear out

phrasal v. 지치게 하다

If you wear someone or yourself out, you make them extremely tired.

descent ^{**}
[disént]

n. 하강, 하락; 가계, 혈통

A descent is a movement from a higher to a lower level or position.

grab ^{복습}
[græb]

v. 부여잡다, 움켜쥐다; n. 부여잡기

If you grab something, you take it or pick it up suddenly and roughly.

unbearable [*]
[ʌnbéərəbəl]

a. 견딜 수 없는, 참을 수 없는

If you describe something as unbearable, you mean that it is so unpleasant, painful, or upsetting that you feel unable to accept it or deal with it.

explosion[**]
[iksplóuʒən]

n. 폭발, 파열
An explosion is a sudden, violent burst of energy, for example one caused by a bomb.

deck[복습]
[dek]

n. 갑판; (카드 패의) 한 벌
A deck on a vehicle such as a bus or ship is a lower or upper area of it.

surround[***]
[səráund]

vt. 둘러싸다, 에워싸다; n. 둘러싸는 것; 환경, 주위
If a person or thing is surrounded by something, that thing is situated all around them.

brilliant[**]
[bríljənt]

a. 빛나는, 찬란한; 훌륭한, 멋진
A brilliant color is extremely bright.

grizzled
[grizld]

a. 회색의, 반백의, 희끗희끗한
A grizzled person or a person with grizzled hair has hair that is grey or partly grey.

paw[복습]
[pɔː]

n. (갈고리 발톱이 있는 동물의) 발; v. 앞발로 차다
The paws of an animal such as a cat, dog, or bear are its feet, which have claws for gripping things and soft pads for walking on.

reckon[복습]
[rékən]

vt. ~라고 생각하다; 세다, 계산하다
If you reckon that something is true, you think that it is true.

whisker[복습]
[wískər]

n. (고양이·쥐 등의) 수염; 구레나룻
The whiskers of an animal such as a cat or a mouse are the long stiff hairs that grow near its mouth.

set something to rights

idiom ~을 고치다, 정돈하다; 바로잡다
If you set or put something to rights, you put it in their right places or right order, or correct it especially one which is unfair.

crate[*]
[kreit]

n. 나무 상자, (짐을 보호하는) 나무틀
A crate is a large box used for transporting or storing things.

position[복습]
[pəzíʃən]

vt. (특정한 장소에) 두다; n. 위치, 자세; 입장, 저지
If you position something somewhere, you put it there carefully, so that it is in the right place or position.

courtesy[복습]
[kə́ːrtisi]

n. 호의; 정중, 친절
If you refer to the courtesy of doing something, you are referring to a polite action.

hearty[**]
[háːrti]

a. 마음에서 우러난, 정성어린 (heartily ad. 진심으로; 열정적으로)
Hearty feelings or opinions are strongly felt or strongly held.

shore[**]
[ʃɔːr]

n. 물가, 강기슭; vt. 상륙시키다
The shores or the shore of a sea, lake, or wide river is the land along the edge of it.

umbrage
[ʌ́mbridʒ]

n. 불쾌(감); 화
If you say that a person takes umbrage, you mean that they are upset or offended by something that someone says or does to them, often without much reason.

refer ^{복습}
[rifə́:r]

v. 언급하다, 나타내다

If you refer to a particular subject or person, you talk about them or mention them.

1분에 몇 단어를 읽는지 리딩 속도를 측정해보세요.

$$\frac{467 \text{ words}}{\text{reading time (} \quad \text{) sec}} \times 60 = (\quad) \text{ WPM}$$

Build Your Vocabulary

light***
[lait]

v. 불을 붙이다. 불이 붙다: 빛을 비추다: n. 빛
If you light something such as a cigarette or fire, or if it lights, it starts burning.

pipe**
[paip]

n. 파이프, 담뱃대: 관, 도관
A pipe is an object which is used for smoking tobacco.

clench*
[klentʃ]

v. (이를) 악물다: (손을) 꽉 쥐다: n. 이를 악물기: 단단히 쥐기
When you clench your teeth or they clench, you squeeze your teeth together firmly, usually because you are angry or upset.

atop
[ətáp]

prep. 꼭대기에, 맨 위에
If something is atop something else, it is on top of it.

conquer**
[káŋkər]

vt. 정복하다
If you conquer something such as a problem, you succeed in ending it or dealing with it successfully.

callused
[kǽləst]

a. (손·발 등의 피부가) 굳어진, 못이 박힌
A foot or hand that is callused is covered in calluses.

blanket**
[blǽŋkit]

v. ~을 (담요로 덮듯이) 전면을 덮다: 담요로 덮다[싸다]: n. 담요, 모포
If something such as snow blankets an area, it covers it.

dusk*
[dʌsk]

n. 땅거미, 황혼, 어스름
Dusk is the time just before night when the daylight has almost gone but when it is not completely dark.

jumble
[dʒʌmbl]

n. 혼잡: 뒤범벅: 주워 모은 것
A jumble of things is a lot of different things that are all mixed together in a disorganized or confused way.

huddle*
[hʌdl]

v. (떼 지어) 몰리다, 움츠리다, 둥글게 말다: n. 군중, 무리
If people huddle together or huddle round something, they stand, sit, or lie close to each other, usually because they all feel cold or frightened.

fellow***
[félou]

n. 녀석, 사나이: 친구, 동료
A fellow is a man or boy.

consider***
[kənsídər]

v. 고려하다, 숙고하다
If you consider something, you think about it carefully.

48

wonder[복습]
[wʌ́ndər]

v. 이상하게 여기다, 호기심을 가지다; n. 경탄할 만한 것, 경이
If you wonder about something, you think about it because it interests you and you want to know more about it.

apron**
[éiprən]

n. 앞치마, 에이프런
An apron is a piece of clothing that you put on over the front of your normal clothes and tie round your waist, especially when you are cooking.

clap[복습]
[klæp]

v. 박수를 치다
When you clap, you hit your hands together to show appreciation or attract attention.

bow[복습]
[bau]

① v. 머리를 숙이다, 굽히다 ② n. 활; 곡선
When you bow, you move your head or the top half of your body forward and downward as a formal way of greeting them or showing respect.

immediately[복습]
[imí:diətli]

ad. 곧 바로, 즉시
If something happens immediately, it happens without any delay.

discerning
[disə́:rniŋ]

a. 통찰력 있는, 식별력 있는
If you describe someone as discerning, you mean that they are able to judge which things of a particular kind are good and which are bad.

confuse**
[kənfjú:z]

v. 어리둥절하게 하다, 혼동하다 (confused a. 당황한, 어리둥절한)
To confuse someone means to make it difficult for them to know exactly what is happening or what to do.

Chapters Nine & Ten

1. What did Nellie do during the day while Lawrence fished?
   A. She watched dramas on TV.
   B. She made furniture.
   C. She visited her friend next door.
   D. She baked in the kitchen.

2. How had Edward's thoughts about people change with Nellie?
   A. He became interested in her stories and started listening.
   B. He became interested in cooking and started carefully watching her bake.
   C. He became more interested in people's jobs.
   D. He became more interested in how people played with dolls.

3. What did the couple do with Edward while they ate dinner?
   A. They put him outside so that he could enjoy fresh air.
   B. They put him in bed so that he could nap.
   C. They put him in a high chair at the table so he could sit with them.
   D. They put a plate of food in front of him to eat.

4. What did Lawrence do with Edward every night after dinner?

    A. He carried Edward on his shoulder and walked through town.

    B. He put him near the window so he could look outside.

    C. He tucked him into a small bed made just for Edward.

    D. He told him a story about his childhood on the sea.

5. What was Lolly's first reaction to Edward?

    A. She wondered why Edward was there and picked him up by one foot.

    B. She thought Edward made her parents happier and liked him.

    C. She completely ignored Edward and didn't notice him.

    D. She thought that it reminded her of a rabbit that she had when she was younger.

6. How did Nellie and Lawrence's behavior toward Edward change when Lolly was around?

    A. They treated Edward like a real child.

    B. They wanted to prepare themselves to give Edward to Lolly.

    C. They ignored Edward and didn't treat him like usual.

    D. They put him on the shelf and treated him like a doll.

7. How did Edward feel when Lolly took him away?

    A. He felt glad that he was going somewhere new and exciting.

    B. He felt pain that he would be separated from Nellie and Lawrence.

    C. He felt that Lolly really cared for Nellie and Lawrence.

    D. He only felt annoyed that his clothes became dirty from the rubbish bin.

1분에 몇 단어를 읽는지 리딩 속도를 측정해보세요.

$$\frac{755 \text{ words}}{\text{reading time } (\quad) \text{ sec}} \times 60 = (\quad) \text{ WPM}$$

Build Your Vocabulary

sew[**]
[sou]

v. 바느질하다, 꿰매다, 깁다
When you sew something such as clothes, you make them or repair them by joining pieces of cloth together by passing thread through them with a needle.

outfit[복습]
[áutfit]

n. 한 벌의 옷, 복장
An outfit is a set of clothes.

ruffle[*]
[rʌfl]

n. 주름 장식, 주름 깃; v. 구기다, 헝클다; (마음을) 흐트러뜨리다
Ruffles are folds of cloth at the neck or the ends of the arms of a piece of clothing, or are sometimes sewn on things as a decoration.

occasion[***]
[əkéiʒən]

n. 경우, 기회; 특별한 일, 행사
An occasion is a time when something happens, or a case of it happening.

fashion[복습]
[fǽʃən]

vt. 만들어내다, 형성하다; n. 유행
If you fashion an object or a work of art, you make it.

cotton[**]
[katn]

n. 솜, 목화
Cotton is a type of cloth made from soft fibers from a particular plant.

strip
[strip]

v. 벗다, 벗기다, 떼어내다; n. 좁고 긴 땅; 길고 가느다란 조각
To strip something means to remove everything that covers it.

horrify[*]
[hɔ́:rəfài]

vt. 충격을 주다, 소름끼치게 하다 (horrified a. 겁에 질린, 충격 받은)
If someone is horrified, they feel shocked or disgusted, because of something that they have seen or heard.

elegant[복습]
[éligənt]

a. 품위 있는, 우아한, 고상한 (elegance n. 우아함, 고상함)
If you describe a person or thing as elegant, you mean that they are pleasing and graceful in appearance or style.

artistry
[á:rtistri]

n. 예술성, 예술적 기교
Artistry is the creative skill of an artist, writer, actor, or musician.

lie[복습]
[lai]

vi. 눕다, 누워 있다; 놓여 있다, 위치하다
If you are lying somewhere, you are in a horizontal position and are not standing or sitting.

muck[복습]
[mʌk]

n. 쓰레기, 오물; 거름, 퇴비; vt. 실패하다, 망쳐놓다
Muck is dirt or some other unpleasant substance.

lean ^{복습}
[li:n]

① v. 기대어 세우다, 기울다; 상체를 굽히다; 기대다, 의지하다 ② a. 야윈, 마른
If you lean an object on or against something, you place the object so that it is partly supported by that thing.

flour***
[flauər]

n. 밀가루; 분말, 가루
Flour is a white or brown powder that is made by grinding grain, which is used to make bread, cakes, and pastry.

canister
[kǽnəstər]

n. 작은 깡통[상자]
A canister is a metal, plastic, or china container with a lid. It is used for storing food such as sugar and flour.

arrange ^{복습}
[əréindʒ]

v. 가지런히 하다, 배열하다; 준비하다
If you arrange things somewhere, you place them in a particular position, usually in order to make them look attractive or tidy.

knead
[ni:d]

vt. 반죽하다; 주무르다, 안마하다
When you knead dough or other food, you press and squeeze it with your hands so that it becomes smooth and ready to cook.

dough
[dou]

n. 반죽 덩어리; 굽지 않은 빵, 가루 반죽
Dough is a fairly firm mixture of flour, water, and sometimes also fat and sugar.

steam**
[sti:m]

v. (창 등이) 증기로 흐리다; 증기가 발생하다; (식품 등을) 찌다; n. 증기
When windows steam up, they become covered with steam.

secretary*
[sékrətèri]

n. 비서, 서기; 사무관, 비서관
A secretary is a person who is employed to do office work, such as typing letters, answering phone calls, and arranging meetings.

drown ^{복습}
[draun]

v. 물에 빠지다, 익사하다; (물에) 빠뜨리다, 익사시키다
When someone drowns or is drowned, they die because they have gone or been pushed under water and cannot breathe.

horrible**
[hɔ́:rəbl]

a. 끔찍한, 소름 끼치는 싫은; 무서운
You can call something horrible when it causes you to feel great shock, fear, and disgust.

suppose ^{복습}
[səpóuz]

v. (~이라고) 생각하다; 가정하다
If you suppose that something is true, you believe that it is probably true, because of other things that you know.

daft
[dæft]

a. 미친 듯한, 어리석은
If you describe a person or their behavior as daft, you think that they are stupid, impractical, or rather strange.

pointless ^{복습}
[pɔ́intlis]

a. 무의미한, 할 가치가 없는
If you say that something is pointless, you are criticizing it because it has no sense or purpose.

strike***
[straik]

v. (struck–struck) 인상[느낌]을 주다; 치다, 찌르다; 습격하다; 충돌하다; n. 공격, 공습; 파업
If something strikes you as being a particular thing, it gives you the impression of being that thing.

somehow[★★]
[sʌ́mhàu]
ad. 여하튼, 어쨌든; 어쩐지, 아무래도
You use somehow to say that you do not know or cannot say how something was done or will be done.

mortify[복습]
[mɔ́:rtəfài]
vt. 굴욕을 느끼게 하다, 분하게 하다
If you say that something mortifies you, you mean that it offends or embarrasses you a great deal.

stare[복습]
[stɛər]
v. 응시하다, 뚫어지게 보다
If you stare at someone or something, you look at them for a long time.

tablecloth[복습]
[téiblklɔ̀:θ]
n. 식탁보, 테이블보
A tablecloth is a cloth used to cover a table.

household[복습]
[háshòuld]
n. (한 집에 사는 사람들을 일컫는) 가정
A household is all the people in a family or group who live together in a house.

light[복습]
[lait]
v. (lit/lighted–lit/lighted) 불을 붙이다, 불이 붙다, 빛을 비추다; n. 빛
If you light something such as a cigarette or fire, or if it lights, it starts burning.

pipe[복습]
[paip]
n. 파이프, 담뱃대; 관, 도관
A pipe is an object which is used for smoking tobacco.

constellation
[kanstəléiʃən]
n. [천문] 별자리, 성좌
A constellation is a group of stars which form a pattern and have a name.

glow[복습]
[glou]
v. 빛을 내다, 빛나다; n. 빛, 밝음
If something glows, it produces a dull, steady light.

chill[★]
[tʃil]
n. 냉기, 한기, 오싹한 느낌; v. 아주 춥게 만들다
If something sends a chill through you, it gives you a sudden feeling of fear or anxiety.

witch[복습]
[witʃ]
n. 마녀
In fairy stories, a witch is a woman, usually an old woman, who has evil magic powers.

lullaby
[lʌ́ləbài]
n. 자장가
A lullaby is a quiet song which is intended to be sung to babies and young children to help them go to sleep.

shine[복습]
[ʃain]
v. 빛나(게 하)다, 반짝이다; n. 빛, 빛남, 광채
Something that shines is very bright and clear because it is reflecting light.

soothe[★]
[su:ð]
v. 달래다, 어르다
If you soothe someone who is angry or upset, you make them feel calmer.

1분에 몇 단어를 읽는지 리딩 속도를 측정해보세요.

$$\frac{438 \text{ words}}{\text{reading time (\quad) sec}} \times 60 = (\quad) \text{ WPM}$$

Build Your Vocabulary

lumpy
[lʌ́mpi]

a. 둔중한, 땅딸막한; 혹투성이의, 울퉁불퉁한
If you describe a person as lumpy, you mean that person is heavy or bulky.

immediately^{복습}
[imíːdiətli]

ad. 곧바로, 즉시
If something happens immediately, it happens without any delay.

spot^{**}
[spat]

vt. 발견하다, 분별하다; n. 반점, 얼룩; 장소, 지점
If you spot something or someone, you notice them.

couch[*]
[kautʃ]

n. 소파, 긴 의자
A couch is a long, comfortable seat for two or three people.

upside down
[ʌ́psàid dáun]

ad. 거꾸로, 뒤집혀
If something has been moved upside down, it has been turned round so that the part that is usually lowest is above the part that is usually highest.

abiding
[əbáidiŋ]

a. 지속적인, 불변의
An abiding feeling, memory, or interest is one that you have for a very long time.

hatred^{**}
[héitrid]

n. 증오, 미움, 원한
Hatred is an extremely strong feeling of dislike for someone or something.

skivvy
[skívi]

n. (구어) 하녀; vi. 허드렛일을 하다
A skivvy is a servant, especially a female, who does menial work of all kinds.

glue[*]
[gluː]

v. ~을 풀[접착제]로 붙이다; 접착하다; n. 풀, 접착제
If you glue one object to another, you stick them together using glue.

lullaby^{복습}
[lʌ́ləbài]

n. 자장가
A lullaby is a quiet song which is intended to be sung to babies and young children to help them go to sleep.

ignore^{**}
[ignɔ́ːr]

vt. 무시하다, 모르는 체하다
If you ignore someone or something, you pay no attention to them.

folk^{***}
[fouk]

n. (pl.) 가족, 부모; (일반적인) 사람들
You can refer to your close family, especially your mother and father, as your folks.

bewitch
[biwítʃ]

vt. 마법을 걸다, 호리다, 매혹시키다
If someone or something bewitches you, you are so attracted to them that you cannot think about anything else.

breeze^{복습}
[bri:z]

n. 산들바람; vi. 산들바람이 불다
A breeze is a gentle wind.

shove^{복습}
[ʃʌv]

v. 밀어넣다, 밀치다, 밀어내다; n. 밀치기
If you shove something somewhere, you push it there quickly and carelessly.

garbage[*]
[gárbidʒ]

n. 쓰레기, 찌꺼기 (garbage can n. 쓰레기통)
Garbage consists of unwanted things or waste material such as used paper, empty tins and bottles, and waste food.

errand^{**}
[érənd]

n. 볼일, 용건; 심부름
An errand is a short trip that you make in order to do a job for someone, for example when you go to a shop to buy something for them.

tremulous
[trémjuləs]

a. (소리·목소리·말이) 떨리는, 떠는
If someone's voice, smile, or actions are tremulous, they are unsteady because the person is uncertain, afraid, or upset.

haul[*]
[hɔ:l]

v. 운반하다; 연행하다, 소환하다; 세게 잡아당기다; n. 운송; 세게 잡아당김
If you haul something which is heavy or difficult to move, you move it using a lot of effort.

1. What gave Edward comfort during his first night at the dump?

   A. There was another doll next to him to keep him company.

   B. He could be found by someone very easily.

   C. He could breathe fresh air.

   D. He could look at the stars.

2. What was the strange ritual that the man Ernest did in the morning at the dump?

   A. He fed a pet crow some of his garbage.

   B. He shouted that he was the king of the world.

   C. He played a song on his harmonica.

   D. He tried to find old toys in the garbage.

3. Why was Edward aware of time passing even after being buried under garbage?

   A. He could still see the sky.

   B. He was buried next to a watch.

   C. Ernest did his morning ritual every day.

   D. He was dug up every day and then buried again.

4. How was Edward discovered in the garbage?
   A. A doll mender searched through the garbage.
   B. A dog dug through the garbage to Edward.
   C. A truck moved the pile of garbage off of Edward.
   D. A child walking by saw Edward and brought him home.

5. How did Edward feel when the dog ran away with him in its mouth?
   A. He felt sad that the dog was ruining his clothing.
   B. He felt disgusted to be in the mouth of a dog.
   C. He felt exhilarated to feel the sunshine again.
   D. He felt scared that the dog was going to eat him.

6. What did Bull say about Edward that made him remember Abilene?
   A. He said that Edward must be missed by some child who loved him.
   B. He said that he had a little daughter with a rabbit doll.
   C. He said that Edward must come from a rich family with a big house.
   D. He said that he would buy a nice pocket watch for Edward.

7. Where did Bull and Lucy live?
   A. They were hoboes and had no home.
   B. They lived next door to Abilene.
   C. They lived in a hotel.
   D. They lived in a cabin in the country.

1분에 몇 단어를 읽는지 리딩 속도를 측정해보세요.

$$\frac{502 \text{ words}}{\text{reading time ( ) sec}} \times 60 = (\qquad) \text{ WPM}$$

Build Your Vocabulary

end up

phrasal v. (구어) 마침내는 (~으로) 되다; 끝나다
If you end up doing something or end up in a particular state, you do that thing or get into that state even though you did not originally intend to.

dump*
[dʌmp]

n. 쓰레기 더미; vt. 내버리다, 쏟아 버리다, 아무렇게나 내려놓다
A dump is a place where rubbish is left, for example on open ground outside a town.

peel*
[piːl]

n. (과일·채소의 두꺼운) 껍질; v. (과일·채소 등의) 껍질을 벗기다
The peel of a fruit such as a lemon or an apple is its skin.

ground***
[graund]

n. (pl.) 찌꺼기; 땅바닥, 지면; a. (가루가 되게) 빻은
Coffee grounds are extremely small pieces of crushed coffee beans, especially after they have been used for making a drink of coffee.

rancid
[rǽnsid]

a. 고약한 냄새가 나는; 불쾌한, (맛이) 고약한
If butter, bacon, or other oily foods are rancid, they have gone bad and taste old and unpleasant.

garbage^{복습}
[gárbidʒ]

n. 쓰레기, 찌꺼기
Garbage consists of unwanted things or waste material such as used paper, empty tins and bottles, and waste food.

heap*
[hiːp]

n. 더미, 쌓아올린 것; 덩어리
A heap of things is a pile of them, especially a pile arranged in a rather untidy way.

comfort^{복습}
[kʌ́mfərt]

n. 마음이 편안함, 안락; 위로, 위안; vt. 위로[위안]하다
If you are doing something in comfort, you are physically relaxed and contented, and are not feeling any pain or other unpleasant sensations.

rubble
[rʌ́bl]

n. (허물어진 건물의) 돌무더기[잔해]
Rubble is used to refer to the small pieces of bricks and stones that are used as a bottom layer on which to build roads, paths, or houses.

armpit
[áːrmpìt]

n. 겨드랑이
Your armpits are the areas of your body under your arms where your arms join your shoulders.

flap**
[flæp]

v. 펄럭이게 하다, 휘날리다, 퍼덕이다; n. 펄럭임, 퍼덕거림
If a bird or insect flaps its wings or if its wings flap, the wings move quickly up and down.

crow[*]
[krou]

① vi. 환성을 지르다, 의기양양해 하다; (수탉이) 울다; n. 수탉의 울음소리
② n. 까마귀

If you say that someone is crowing about something they have achieved or are pleased about, you disapprove of them because they keep telling people proudly about it.

therefore[***]
[ðέərfɔ́:r]

ad. 그러므로, 그러니

You use therefore to introduce a logical result or conclusion.

incline[**]
[inkláin]

v. 마음이 기울게 하다, ~하고 싶어지다; 기울다, 기울어지게 하다; n. 경사, 비탈
(inclined a. 마음 내키는, 하고 싶은)

If you incline to think or act in a particular way, or if something inclines you to it, you are likely to think or act in that way.

assess[*]
[əsés]

vt. 평가하다; 부과하다, 매기다 (assessment n. 평가, 부과, 과세)

When you assess a person, thing, or situation, you consider them in order to make a judgment about them.

load[***]
[loud]

n. 한 짐(의 분량), 다수, 다량; 적재 화물, 짐; v. 짐을 싣다

If you refer to a load of people or things or loads of them, you are emphasizing that there are a lot of them.

deposit[*]
[dipázit]

vt. 두다, 놓다; 맡기다, 예금하다

To deposit something somewhere means to put them or leave them there.

bury[**]
[béri]

vt. 묻다, 파묻다, 매장하다

To bury something means to put it into a hole in the ground and cover it up with earth.

exact[복습]
[igzǽkt]

v. (남에게 나쁜 일을) 가하다[일으키다]; 받아 내다, 요구하다; a. 정확한, 정밀한

If someone exacts revenge on a person, they have their revenge on them.

revenge[*]
[rivéndʒ]

n. 복수, 보복; vt. 복수하다, 원수를 갚다

Revenge involves hurting or punishing someone who has hurt or harmed you.

give up

phrasal v. 포기하다, 단념하다

If you give up, you decide that you cannot do something and stop trying to do it.

give in

phrasal v. 굴복하다, 따르다, 항복하다

If you give in, you admit that you are defeated or that you cannot do something.

despair[**]
[dispέər]

n. 절망, 자포자기; vi. 절망하다

Despair is the feeling that everything is wrong and that nothing will improve.

witch[복습]
[witʃ]

n. 마녀

In fairy stories, a witch is a woman, usually an old woman, who has evil magic powers.

aware[**]
[əwéər]

a. 알고 있는, 의식하고 있는, 알아차린

If you are aware of something, you know about it.

dawn^{복습}
[dɔːn]

n. 새벽, 동틀 녘; vi. 날이 새다, 밝아지다; 나타나기 시작하다
Dawn is the time of day when light first appears in the sky, just before the sun rises.

ritual[*]
[rítʃuəl]

n. (종교적인) 의식, 행사
A ritual is a religious service or other ceremony which involves a series of actions performed in a fixed order.

cackle
[kǽkl]

v. (불쾌하게) 낄낄 웃다, 키득거리다; 꼬꼬댁 울다
If someone cackles, they laugh in a loud unpleasant way, often at something bad that happens to someone else.

salvation
[sælvéiʃən]

n. 구제, 구출, 보호
The salvation of someone or something is the act of saving them from harm, destruction, or an unpleasant situation.

unusual^{복습}
[ʌnjúːʒuəl]

a. 보통이 아닌, 예외적인, 드문
If something is unusual, it does not happen very often or you do not see it or hear it very often.

shift[*]
[ʃift]

① v. 옮기다, 이동하다; n. 교대 근무; 교체, 순환 ② n. [의복] 시프트 드레스
If you shift something or if it shifts, it moves slightly.

sniff^{복습}
[snif]

v. 킁킁거리다, 냄새를 맡다; 콧방귀를 뀌다; n. 냄새 맡음; 콧방귀
If you sniff something or sniff at it, you smell it by sniffing.

pant^{**}
[pænt]

vi. 헐떡거리다, 숨차다; n. 헐떡거림, 숨 가쁨
If you pant, you breathe quickly and loudly with your mouth open, because you have been doing something energetic.

frenzy[*]
[frénzi]

vi. 격분[광란]하게 하다; n. 격분, 광란 (frenzied a. 광적인, 제정신이 아닌)
Frenzied activities or actions are wild, excited, and uncontrolled.

miraculous[*]
[mirǽkjuləs]

a. 놀랄 만한, 기적적인, 초자연적인 (miraculously ad. 놀랄 만하게, 기적적으로)
If you describe a good event as miraculous, you mean that it is very surprising and unexpected.

62

1분에 몇 단어를 읽는지 리딩 속도를 측정해보세요.

$$\frac{594 \ words}{reading \ time \ (\quad) \ sec} \times 60 = (\quad) \ WPM$$

Build Your Vocabulary

savor[*]
[séivər]
v. 맛보다, 음미하다; n. 맛, 풍미
If you savor an experience, you enjoy it as much as you can.

shaggy[*]
[ʃǽgi]
a. 덥수룩한, 털이 많은
Shaggy hair or fur is long and untidy.

a great deal of
idiom 다량의
If you say that you need or have a great deal of or a good deal of a particular thing, you are emphasizing that you need or have a lot of it.

ferocity[복습]
[fərásəti]
n. 흉포함; 흉포한 행동
The ferocity of something is its fierce or violent nature.

growl[복습]
[graul]
v. 으르렁거리다; n. 으르렁거리는 소리
When a dog or other animal growls, it makes a low noise in its throat, usually because it is angry.

throat[**]
[θrout]
n. 목, 목구멍; 좁은 통로
Your throat is the back of your mouth and the top part of the tubes that go down into your stomach and your lungs.

stare[복습]
[stɛər]
v. 응시하다, 뚫어지게 보다
If you stare at someone or something, you look at them for a long time.

garbage[복습]
[gárbidʒ]
n. 쓰레기, 찌꺼기
Garbage consists of unwanted things or waste material such as used paper, empty tins and bottles, and waste food.

therefore[복습]
[ðɛ́ərfɔ̀ːr]
ad. 그러므로, 그러니
You use therefore to introduce a logical result or conclusion.

grab[복습]
[græb]
v. 부여잡다, 움켜쥐다; n. 부여잡기
If you grab something, you take it or pick it up suddenly and roughly.

exhilarate
[igzílərèit]
vt. 기분을 들뜨게 하다, 유쾌하게 하다 (exhilarated a. 마음이 들떠 있는, 유쾌한)
If you are exhilarated by something, it makes you feel very happy and excited.

crust[**]
[krʌst]
vt. ~에 겉껍질이 생기게 하다; n. 딱딱한 표면, 겉껍질
If something is crusted with a substance, it is covered with a hard or thick layer of that substance.

slobbery
[slábəri]

a. 군침을 흘리는, 침으로 젖은; 축축한
Something slobbery is wet in an unpleasant way.

chase**
[tʃeis]

v. 쫓아가다, 추격하다; n. 추적, 추구
If you chase someone, or chase after them, you run after them or follow them quickly in order to catch or reach them.

scraggly
[skrǽgli]

a. (수염 따위가) 터부룩한, 삐죽삐죽한, 우툴두툴한
Scraggly hair or plants are thin and untidy.

bush**
[buʃ]

n. 관목(숲), 덤불; v. 무성해지다, 뒤덮다
A bush is a large plant which is smaller than a tree and has a lot of branches.

attach**
[ətǽtʃ]

vt. 붙이다, 달다 (attached a. 붙여진)
If you attach something to an object, you connect it or fasten it to the object.

enormous**
[inɔ́ːrməs]

a. 엄청난, 거대한, 막대한
You can use enormous to emphasize the great degree or extent of something.

beard**
[biərd]

n. (턱)수염
A man's beard is the hair that grows on his chin and cheeks.

firm***
[fəːrm]

① a. 굳은, 단단한; 견고한 (firmly ad. 굳게) ② n. 회사
If someone's grip is firm or if they perform a physical action in a firm way, they do it with quite a lot of force or pressure but also in a controlled way.

delight***
[diláit]

n. 기쁨, 즐거움; v. 즐겁게 하다, 매우 기쁘게 하다
Delight is a feeling of very great pleasure.

existence^{복습}
[igzístəns]

n. 존재, 실재, 현존
The existence of something is the fact that it is present in the world as a real thing.

yip
[jip]

n. 깽깽 짖는 소리; v. (강아지 등이) 깽깽 짖다
If a dog or other animal yips, it gives a sudden short cry, often because of fear or pain.

gracious**
[gréiʃəs]

a. 정중한, 품위 있는, 우아한 (graciously ad. 정중하게)
If you describe the behavior of someone in a position of authority as gracious, you mean that they behave in a polite and considerate way.

definitely**
[défənitli]

ad. 명확히, 확실히
You use definitely to emphasize that something is the case, or to emphasize the strength of your intention or opinion.

hard-pressed
[hard-prest]

a. ～을 하는 데 애를 먹는; (일·돈·시간에) 쪼들리는
If you will be hard-pressed to do something, you will have great difficulty doing it.

chef
[ʃef]

n. 주방장, 요리사
A chef is a cook in a restaurant or hotel.

64

separate[***]
[sépəreit]

v. 가르다, 떼다, 분리하다 (separated a. 분리가 된)
If you separate people or things that are together, or if they separate, they move apart.

lead[복습]
[li:d]

① vt. 인도하다, 이끌다, 인솔하다; n. 선도, 솔선, 지휘 ② n. [광물] 납
If a road, gate, or door leads somewhere, you can get there by following the road or going through the gate or door.

dusk[복습]
[dʌsk]

n. 땅거미, 황혼, 어스름
Dusk is the time just before night when the daylight has almost gone but when it is not completely dark.

descend[**]
[disénd]

v. (어둠·땅거미 등이) 내려앉다, 깔리다, 다가오다, 엄습하다; 내려가다
When night, dusk, or darkness descends, it starts to get dark.

agreeable[*]
[əgrí:əbl]

a. 기분 좋은; (사람이) 쾌활한; 선뜻 동의하는
If something is agreeable, it is pleasant and you enjoy it.

company[***]
[kʌ́mpəni]

n. 사귐, 교제; 동료, 친구; 회사; v. 따르다, 동행하다
(in the company of idiom ~와 함께)
Company is having another person or other people with you, usually when this is pleasant or stops you feeling lonely.

surmise
[sərmáiz]

vt. 추측하다, 짐작하다
If you surmise that something is true, you guess it from the available evidence, although you do not know for certain.

care[***]
[kɛər]

vi. ~하고 싶어하다, 좋아하다; 돌보다; 걱정하다, 염려하다; n. 돌봄; 주의, 유의
You can ask someone if they would care for something or if they would care to do something as a polite way of asking if they would like to have or do something.

nod[복습]
[nad]

v. 끄덕이다, 끄덕여 표시하다; n. (동의·인사·신호·명령의) 끄덕임
If you nod, you move your head downward and upward to show agreement, understanding, or approval.

swell[*]
[swel]

a. 아주 좋은, 멋진; v. (가슴이) 벅차다; 부풀다, 팽창하다; n. 팽창, 증대
You can describe something as swell if you think it is really nice.

wag[*]
[wæg]

v. (꼬리 등을) 흔들다, 흔들리다; n. 흔들기
When a dog wags its tail, it repeatedly waves its tail from side to side.

take to the road

idiom 여행에 나서다, 방랑자가 되다
Taking to the road means to start on a journey.

hobo
[hóubou]

n. 부랑자, 떠돌이
A hobo is a person who has no home, especially one who travels from place to place and gets money by begging.

Chapters Thirteen & Fourteen

1. Where were Bull and Lucy traveling to with Edward?
   A. They were actually going nowhere.
   B. They were going to Memphis.
   C. They were going to the sea to take a ship to London.
   D. They were going to take him back to Abilene.

2. How did Edward's feelings toward Lucy change?
   A. He felt braver around her because she protected him.
   B. He still felt a little afraid of her from their first meeting.
   C. He hated her because he had bad experience with dogs.
   D. He felt tenderness for her after she curled around him when she slept.

3. What did Edward say to himself when he looked at the stars?
   A. He said the constellation names and then the names of those he loved.
   B. He said the North Star will guide him to Abilene.
   C. He said that he wished he could fly to the stars.
   D. He said the name of constellations that looked like animals.

4. After Bull made new clothes for Edward, what did he say Edward looked like?

A. He said Edward looked like an orphan and a sad rabbit.

B. He said Edward looked like an outcast and a lonely rabbit.

C. He said Edward looked like an outlaw and a rabbit on the run.

D. He said Edward looked like a doctor and a smart rabbit.

5. At first the other men that Bull met made fun of Edward, but how did they feel about him after time passed?

A. They became annoyed with Edward and ignored him.

B. They became accustomed to Edward and recognized him.

C. They became scared of Edward because they thought Bull was crazy.

D. They became shy around Edward because he reminded them of their childhood toys.

6. What would some of the hoboes whisper to Edward?

A. They would whisper the names of their children.

B. They would whisper the names of their wives.

C. They would whisper the names of their old friends.

D. They would whisper the names of the constellations.

7. How did Edward become separated from Bull and Lucy?

A. Another hobo stole Edward while they both slept.

B. Another dog carried Edward away just like Lucy had done with him.

C. They simply forgot about Edward one day and left him behind.

D. A man on a freight car kicked Edward out of the train.

1분에 몇 단어를 읽는지 리딩 속도를 측정해보세요.

$$\frac{585 \text{ words}}{\text{reading time (} \qquad \text{) sec}} \times 60 = (\qquad) \text{ WPM}$$

Build Your Vocabulary

irony[*]
[áiərəni]

n. 반어, 아이러니
If you talk about the irony of a situation, you mean that it is odd or amusing because it involves a contrast.

constant[*]
[kánstənt]

a. 끊임없는, 일정한, 불변의
You use constant to describe something that happens all the time or is always there.

bedroll
[bédròul]

n. 휴대용 침구, 침낭
A bedroll is a rolled-up sleeping bag or other form of bedding, which you can carry with you.

sling[*]
[sliŋ]

vt. (slung–slung) 던져 올리다, 걸치다; 투석기로 쏘다
If you sling something over your shoulder or over something such as a chair, you hang it there loosely.

stick out

phrasal v. 불쑥 나오다, 돌출하다
If something sticks out, it is further out than something else.

position^{복습}
[pəzíʃən]

vt. (특정한 장소에) 두다; n. 위치, 자세; 입장, 처지
If you position something somewhere, you put it there carefully, so that it is in the right place or position.

initial^{복습}
[iníʃəl]

a. 처음의, 최초의; n. 이니셜, 머리글자
You use initial to describe something that happens at the beginning of a process.

fit^{복습}
[fit]

① a. 알맞은, 적합한; v. 꼭 맞다, 어울리다 (unfit a. 부적합한) ② n. 발작, 경련
If something fits, it is the right size and shape to go onto a person's body or onto a particular object.

consumption^{**}
[kənsʌ́mpʃən]

n. 소비(량), 소모, 소진
The consumption of food or drink is the act of eating or drinking something, or the amount that is eaten or drunk.

liking[*]
[láikiŋ]

n. 좋아하기; 취미, 기호
If you have a liking for something or someone, you like them.

curl^{**}
[kə:rl]

v. 몸을 웅크리다; 감(기)다; 곱슬하다; n. 곱슬머리, 동그랗게 말리는 것
If you curl up, you lie down or sit down with your back curved and your knees and arms close to your body.

muzzle
[mʌzl]

n. (동물의) 주둥이, 부리; 총구, 포구; vt. 재갈 물리다, 말 못하게 하다
The muzzle of an animal such as a dog is its nose and mouth.

whimper[*]
[hwímpər]

v. 낑낑거리다; 훌쩍이다, 울먹이다
If someone whimpers, they make quiet unhappy or frightened sounds, as if they are about to start crying.

growl[복습]
[graul]

v. 으르렁거리다; n. 으르렁거리는 소리
When a dog or other animal growls, it makes a low noise in its throat, usually because it is angry.

chuff
[tʃʌf]

v. 식식 소리를 내다; n. 식식 하는 소리
That someone chuff means they make a puffing sound or a sound of a steam engine.

resonate
[rézənèit]

v. 울려 퍼지다; 공명(공진)하다
If something resonates, it vibrates and produces a deep, strong sound.

tenderness[**]
[téndərnis]

n. 다정, 친절; 유연함; 마음이 무름
A tenderness is a tendency to express warm and affectionate feeling.

constellation[복습]
[kanstəléiʃən]

n. [천문] 별자리, 성좌
A constellation is a group of stars which form a pattern and have a name.

gather[***]
[gǽðər]

v. 모이다, 집결하다; 모으다, 끌다
If people gather somewhere or if someone gathers people somewhere, they come together in a group.

tramp[*]
[træmp]

n. 방랑자; 도보 여행; 발걸음 (소리), 쿵쿵거리기; v. 방랑하다; 쿵쿵거리며 걷다
A tramp is a person who has no home or job, and very little money. Tramps go from place to place, and get food or money by asking people or by doing casual work.

lean[복습]
[li:n]

① v. 기울다, 기대어 세우다; 상체를 굽히다; 기대다, 의지하다 ② a. 야윈, 마른
If you lean an object on or against something, you place the object so that it is partly supported by that thing.

sense[***]
[sens]

vt. 느끼다, 알아채다; n. 느낌, 기분; 감각
If you sense something, you become aware of it or you realize it, although it is not very obvious.

offend[**]
[əfénd]

v. 불쾌하게 하다, 성나게 하다; 죄를 범하다
If you offend someone, you say or do something rude which upsets or embarrasses them.

comment[**]
[káment]

v. 의견을 말하다, 논평하다; n. 주석, 논평
If you comment on something, you give your opinion about it or you give an explanation for it.

negative[***]
[négətiv]

a. 부정적인, 비판적인; 소극적인 (negatively ad. 부정적으로)
If someone is negative or has a negative attitude, they consider only the bad aspects of a situation, rather than the good ones.

garb
[ga:rb]

n. 의복, 옷차림; 외모, 외관
Someone's garb is the clothes they are wearing, especially when these are unusual.

force^{복습}
[fɔ:rs]

vt. 강요하다, 억지로 밀어 넣다; n. 힘, 폭력; 군사력, 병력
If someone forces you to do something, they make you do it even though you do not want to, for example by threatening you.

sore^{**}
[sɔ:r]

a. 아픈, 쓰린
If part of your body is sore, it causes you pain and discomfort.

fare^{**}
[fɛər]

vi. (일이) 되어 가다; (사람이) 해 나가다; n. 요금, 운임
If you say that someone or something fares well or badly, you are referring to the degree of success they achieve in a particular situation or activity.

dump^{복습}
[dʌmp]

n. 쓰레기 더미; vt. 내버리다, 쏟아 버리다, 아무렇게나 내려놓다
A dump is a place where rubbish is left, for example on open ground outside a town.

subsequent[*]
[sʌ́bsikwənt]

a. 다음의, 그 후의, 이어서 일어나는
You use subsequent to describe something that happened or existed after the time or event that has just been referred to.

ramble[*]
[ræmbl]

vi. 정처없이 거닐다, 어슬렁거리다, 산책하다; 구불구불 뻗어가다; n. 산책, 만보
If you ramble, you go on a long walk in the countryside.

tear^{**}
[tɛər]

① v. (tore-torn) 찢(어지)다; 부리나케 가다; n. 찢음 ② n. 눈물
If you tear paper, cloth, or another material, or if it tears, you pull it into two pieces or you pull it so that a hole appears in it.

barely^{복습}
[bέərli]

ad. 거의 ~없게; 간신히, 가까스로
You use barely to say that something is only just true or only just the case.

resemble[*]
[rizémbl]

vt. ~을 닮다, ~와 공통점이 있다
If one thing or person resembles another, they are similar to each other.

approval^{**}
[əprúːvəl]

n. 찬성, 동의; 승인
Approval is a formal or official statement that something is acceptable.

knit^{**}
[nit]

v. (knit-knit) 뜨다, 짜다; (눈살을) 찌푸리다
If you knit something, especially an article of clothing, you make it from wool or a similar thread by using two knitting needles or a machine.

embarrass^{복습}
[imbǽrəs]

v. 부끄럽게[무안하게] 하다; 당황하다
If something or someone embarrasses you, they make you feel shy or ashamed.

naked^{복습}
[néikid]

a. 나체의, 발가벗은; 적나라한 (nakedness n. 발가벗음; 솔직함)
Someone who is naked is not wearing any clothes.

slide[*]
[slaid]

v. (slid-slid) (물건을) ~에 슬쩍 집어넣다; 미끄러지다, 미끄러지듯 움직이다
When something slides somewhere or when you slide it there, it moves there smoothly over or against something.

poke[*]
[pouk]

v. 쑥 내밀다; (손가락 등으로) 쿡 찌르다; n. 찌르기[쑤시기]
If something pokes out of or through another thing, you can see part of it appearing from behind or underneath the other thing.

handkerchief**
[hǽŋkərtʃif]

n. 손수건
A handkerchief is a small square piece of fabric which you use for blowing your nose.

sew**복습
[sou]

v. 바느질하다, 꿰매다, 깁다
When you sew something such as clothes, you make them or repair them by joining pieces of cloth together by passing thread through them with a needle.

makeshift*
[méikʃift]

a. 임시변통의, 일시적인; n. 임시 수단, 미봉책
Makeshift things are temporary and usually of poor quality, but they are used because there is nothing better available.

outlaw
[áutlɔ̀ː]

n. 범법자; vt. 불법화하다, 금지하다
An outlaw is a criminal who is hiding from the authorities.

admire**
[ædmáiər]

v. 감탄하며 바라보다; 존경하다, 칭찬하다
If you admire someone or something, you like and respect them very much.

on the run

a. 도망을 다니는, 도주 중인; 계속 돌아다니는
If someone is on the run, they are running away or hiding from the police.

1분에 몇 단어를 읽는지 리딩 속도를 측정해보세요.

$$\frac{861 \text{ words}}{\text{reading time (} \qquad \text{) sec}} \times 60 = (\qquad) \text{ WPM}$$

Build Your Vocabulary

hobo 복습
[hóubou]
n. 부랑자, 떠돌이
A hobo is a person who has no home, especially one who travels from place to place and gets money by begging.

chop *
[tʃap]
vt. 자르다, 잘게 썰다; n. 잘라낸 조각; 절단
If you chop something, you cut it into pieces with strong downward movements of a knife or an axe.

surge *
[sə:rdʒ]
n. 격동, (파도 같은) 쇄도, 돌진; v. 쇄도하다, 밀어닥치다
A surge is a sudden large increase in something that has previously been steady, or has only increased or developed slowly.

refer 복습
[rifɔ́:r]
v. 언급하다, 나타내다
If you refer to a particular subject or person, you talk about them or mention them.

accustom **
[əkʌ́stəm]
v. 익히다, 익숙해지다 (accustomed a. 익숙해진)
If you accustom yourself or another person to something, you make yourself or them become used to it.

existence 복습
[igzístəns]
n. 존재, 실재, 현존
The existence of something is the fact that it is present in the world as a real thing.

spread 복습
[spred]
v. 퍼지다, 펴다, 펼치다; 뿌리다; n. 퍼짐, 폭, 넓이
If something spreads or is spread by people, it gradually reaches or affects a larger and larger area or more and more people.

entire 복습
[intáiər]
a. 전체의; 완전한 (entirely ad. 완전히)
You use entire when you want to emphasize that you are referring to the whole of something, for example, the whole of a place, time, or population.

unison *
[jú:nəsən]
n. 조화, 화합, 일치 (in unison idiom 일제히)
If people do something in unison, they do the same thing at the same time.

rush 복습
[rʌʃ]
n. 쇄도; 돌진; v. 돌진하다, 급히 움직이다, 서두르다
If you experience a rush of a feeling, you suddenly experience it very strongly.

recognize ***
[rékəgnaiz]
vt. 인지하다, 알아보다
If you recognize someone or something, you know who that person is or what that thing is.

ability[**]
[əbíləti]

n. 능력, 재능
Your ability to do something is the fact that you can do it.

concentrate[**]
[kánsəntrèit]

v. 집중하다, 전념하다
If you concentrate on something, you give all your attention to it.

invaluable
[invǽljuəbəl]

a. 값을 헤아릴 수 없는, 매우 귀중한, 평가할 수 없는
If you describe something as invaluable, you mean that it is extremely useful.

borrow[***]
[bárou]

v. 빌리다, 차용하다
If you borrow something that belongs to someone else, you take it or use it for a period of time, usually with their permission.

whisper[복습]
[hwíspə:r]

v. 속삭이다
When you whisper, you say something very quietly.

tramp[복습]
[træmp]

n. 방랑자; 도보 여행; 발걸음 (소리), 쿵쿵거리기; v. 방랑하다; 쿵쿵거리며 걷다
A tramp is a person who has no home or job, and very little money. Tramps go from place to place, and get food or money by asking people or by doing casual work.

aside[*]
[əsáid]

ad. 한쪽으로; (길을) 비켜
If you take or draw someone aside, you take them a little way away from a group of people in order to talk to them in private.

restless[**]
[réstlis]

a. 가만히 못 있는; 침착하지 못한; 쉬지 못하는, 불안한
If someone is restless, they keep moving around because they find it difficult to keep still.

soothe[복습]
[su:ð]

v. 달래다, 어르다
If you soothe someone who is angry or upset, you make them feel calmer.

freight[*]
[freit]

n. 화물, 화물 운송; v. 운송하다
Freight is the movement of goods by trains, ships, or airplanes.

shine[복습]
[ʃain]

v. (shone–shone) 빛나(게 하)다, 반짝이다; n. 빛, 빛남, 광채
Something that shines is very bright and clear because it is reflecting light.

flashlight[*]
[flǽʃlait]

n. 손전등, 회중전등
A flashlight is a small electric light which gets its power from batteries and which you can carry in your hand.

bum
[bʌm]

n. 부랑자, 게으름뱅이
A bum is a person who has no permanent home or job and who gets money by working occasionally or by asking people for money.

swift[*]
[swift]

a. 빠른, 신속한
A swift event or process happens very quickly or without delay.

yelp
[jelp]

v. 깽깽 짖다; 큰소리로 말하다; n. 깽깽 우는 소리, (개가 성내어) 짖는 소리
If a person or dog yelps, they give a sudden short cry, often because of fear or pain.

bendable ^{복습}
[béndəbl]
a. 구부릴 수 있는; 융통성이 있는
A bendable object or material is capable of being bent or twisted without breaking.

defend[*]
[difénd]
v. 방어하다, 지키다
If you defend someone or something, you take action in order to protect them.

lie ^{복습}
[lai]
vi. 눕다, 누워 있다; 놓여 있다, 위치하다
If you are lying somewhere, you are in a horizontal position and are not standing or sitting.

bet[*]
[bet]
v. 틀림없다, ~라고 확신하다; 걸다, 내기를 하다; n. 내기, 내기돈
You use expressions such as 'I bet', 'I'll bet', and 'you can bet' to indicate that you are sure something is true.

poke ^{복습}
[pouk]
v. (손가락 등으로) 쿡 찌르다; 쑥 내밀다; n. 찌르기[쑤시기]
If you poke someone or something, you quickly push them with your finger or with a sharp object.

watch^{***}
[watʃ]
n. 감시, 경계; 관찰, 주시; 손목시계; v. 지켜보다, 주시하다; 기다리다; 돌보다
If someone is on watch, they have the job of carefully looking and listening, often while other people are asleep and often as a military duty, so that they can warn them of danger or an attack.

charge^{**}
[tʃa:rdʒ]
n. 책임, 의무; 요금; 고발, 비난; v. 맡기다, 담당시키다; 청구하다; 고발하다
If you are in charge in a particular situation, you are the most senior person and have control over something or someone.

lurch
[lə:rtʃ]
v. 휘청하다, 요동치다, 비틀거리다
To lurch means to make a sudden movement, especially forwards, in an uncontrolled way.

fling ^{복습}
[fliŋ]
vt. (flung-flung) (문 등을) 왈칵 열다; 내던지다, 던지다
If you fling something somewhere, you throw it there using a lot of force.

anguish[*]
[ǽŋgwiʃ]
v. 괴로워하다, 괴롭히다; n. 괴로움, 고뇌, 번민 (anguished a. 괴로움이 가득찬)
Anguish is great mental suffering or physical pain.

howl[*]
[haul]
n. 울부짖는 소리; v. 짖다, 울부짖다
A howl is a long, loud, crying sound.

thump[*]
[θʌmp]
n. 탁[쿵] 하는 소리; 때림, 세게 쥐어박음; v. 부딪치다
A thump is a loud, dull sound by hitting something.

tumble ^{복습}
[tʌmbl]
v. 굴러 떨어지다, 넘어지다; n. 추락, 폭락
If someone or something tumbles somewhere, they fall there with a rolling or bouncing movement.

stare ^{복습}
[stɛər]
v. 응시하다, 뚫어지게 보다
If you stare at someone or something, you look at them for a long time.

wonder ^{복습}
[wʌ́ndər]
v. 이상하게 여기다, 호기심을 가지다; n. 경탄할 만한 것, 경이
If you wonder about something, you think about it because it interests you and you want to know more about it.

74

cricket[*]
[kríkit]

n. [곤충] 귀뚜라미

A cricket is a brown or black insect which makes short loud noises by rubbing its wings together.

ache^{복습}
[eik]

vi. 쑤시다, 아프다; n. 아픔, 쑤심

If you ache or a part of your body aches, you feel a steady, fairly strong pain.

1. How did Edward feel when the woman found him in the road?

   A. He felt that she was actually Pellegrina.

   B. He felt glad that someone found him so quickly.

   C. He felt that she would be kind since she reminded him of Nellie.

   D. He felt it didn't make a difference whether or not she picked him up.

2. When the woman found Edward, what use did she have for him?

   A. She used Edward to comfort her son, Bryce.

   B. She used him for decoration on her farm.

   C. She put Edward on a post to scare away birds.

   D. She used him to entertain the local children.

3. What name did the woman give to Edward?

   A. Claire

   B. Clyde

   C. Clint

   D. Clarence

4. Why did looking at the stars not bring Edward comfort as usual?

A. He felt that they mocked him for being alone.

B. He felt that they were so far away.

C. He imagined that they were cold in space.

D. He got a headache from trying to count them all.

5. Why was the woman yelling at the boy?

A. He was trying to steal Edward in front of her.

B. He was throwing rocks at Edward.

C. He was looking at Edward instead of working.

D. He was late for work again.

6. Which of the following was something Edward did NOT say he would do if he had had wings?

A. He would have flown into the sky when thrown overboard on the ship.

B. He would have flown out of the dump when Lolly brought him there.

C. He would have flown out of the train when the man kicked him.

D. He would have flown as high as he could to be with the stars forever.

7. How did Edward feel when Bryce came back for him?

A. He felt relief and joy for being saved.

B. He felt upset because he liked being alone.

C. He felt sad because he thought that Bryce would leave him.

D. He felt nervous because Bryce looked scary.

1분에 몇 단어를 읽는지 리딩 속도를 측정해보세요.

$$\frac{624 \text{ words}}{\text{reading time } (\quad) \text{ sec}} \times 60 = (\quad) \text{ WPM}$$

Build Your Vocabulary

cricket ^{복습}
[kríkit]

n. [곤충] 귀뚜라미
A cricket is a brown or black insect which makes short loud noises by rubbing its wings together.

give way ^{복습}

idiom (~에게) 양보하다
If one thing gives way to another, the first thing is replaced by the second.

trip***
[trip]

v. 걸려 넘어지다; 경쾌한 걸음걸이로 걷다; n. 여행
If you trip when you are walking, you knock your foot against something and fall or nearly fall.

pole***
[poul]

n. 막대, 기둥; 극 (fishing pole n. 낚싯대)
A pole is a long thin piece of wood or metal, used especially for supporting things.

rub**
[rʌb]

v. 쓰다듬다; 문지르다, 맞비비다; 닦다, 윤내다; n. 닦기, 마찰
If you rub a part of your body, you move your hand or fingers backward and forward over it while pressing firmly.

ache ^{복습}
[eik]

n. 아픔, 쑤심; vi. 쑤시다, 아프다
An ache is a steady, fairly strong pain in a part of your body.

replace**
[ripléis]

v. 대신하다, 대체하다
If one thing or person replaces another, the first is used or acts instead of the second.

hollow***
[hálou]

a. 공허한; 속이 빈; 오목한; n. 구멍; 움푹한 곳; v. 속이 비다 (hollowness n. 공허)
If you describe a statement, situation, or person as hollow, you mean they have no real value, worth, or effectiveness.

despair ^{복습}
[dispéər]

n. 절망, 자포자기; vi. 절망하다
Despair is the feeling that everything is wrong and that nothing will improve.

weed*
[wi:d]

n. 잡초; v. 잡초를 없애다
A weed is a wild plant that grows in gardens or fields of crops and prevents the plants that you want from growing properly.

swing**
[swiŋ]

v. 휘두르다, (한 점을 축으로 하여) 빙 돌다, 홱 움직이다
If something swings or if you swing it, it moves repeatedly backward and forward or from side to side from a fixed point.

in spite of
idiom ~에도 불구하고, ~을 무릅쓰고 (inspite of oneself idiom 자기도 모르게)
If you say that someone did something in spite of a fact, you mean it is surprising that that fact did not prevent them from doing it.

bet^{복습}
[bet]
v. 틀림없다, ~라고 확신하다; 걸다, 내기를 하다; n. 내기, 내기돈
You use expressions such as 'I bet', 'I'll bet', and 'you can bet' to indicate that you are sure something is true.

apparent[*]
[əpǽrənt]
a. 또렷한, 명백한; 외관상의 (apparently ad. 보아하니, 명백히)
If something is apparent to you, it is clear and obvious to you.

hang^{복습}
[hæŋ]
v. 걸다, 달아매다; 매달리다, 달려 있다; 배회하다; 교수형에 처하다
If something hangs in a high place or position, or if you hang it there, it is attached there so it does not touch the ground.

nail^{***}
[neil]
vt. 못을 박다; n. 못; 손톱, 발톱
If you nail something somewhere, you fix it there using one or more nails.

attach^{복습}
[ətǽtʃ]
vt. 붙이다, 달다
If you attach something to an object, you connect it or fasten it to the object.

paw^{복습}
[pɔː]
n. (갈고리 발톱이 있는 동물의) 발; v. 앞발로 차다
The paws of an animal such as a cat, dog, or bear are its feet, which have claws for gripping things and soft pads for walking on.

wire^{복습}
[wáiər]
n. 철사; 전선, 케이블; v. 철사로 매다; 전송하다, 전보로 알리다
A wire is a long thin piece of metal that is used to fasten things or to carry electric current.

tin^{**}
[tin]
n. 양철 깡통[냄비], 주석
A tin is a metal container which is filled with food and sealed in order to preserve the food for long periods of time.

clink
[kliŋk]
v. 땡땡 울리다[소리나게 하다]; n. (유리 등의) 땡그랑 소리
If objects clink or if you clink them, they touch each other and make a short, light sound.

clank^{복습}
[klæŋk]
v. 철커덕 하는 소리가 나다; n. 철커덕 (소리)
When large metal objects clank, they make a noise because they are hitting together or hitting against something hard.

shine^{복습}
[ʃain]
v. (shone–shone) 빛나(게 하)다, 반짝이다; n. 빛, 빛남, 광채
Something that shines is very bright and clear because it is reflecting light.

crow^{복습}
[krou]
① n. 까마귀 ② vi. (수탉이) 울다; n. 수탉의 울음소리
A crow is a large black bird which makes a loud, harsh noise.

caw
[kɔː]
vi. 까악까악 울다; n. (의성어) 까악까악 (새의 울음 소리)
When a bird such as a crow or a rook caws, it makes a loud harsh sound.

screech[*]
[skriːtʃ]
v. 끼익 소리 나(게 하)다; 새된 소리를 지르다; n. 날카로운 외침
When a bird, animal, or thing screeches, it makes a loud, unpleasant, high-pitched noise.

wheel***
[hwi:l]

v. 선회하다, 방향을 바꾸다; 움직이다, 밀다; n. 수레바퀴; 핸들
If something such as a group of animals or birds wheels, it moves in a circle.

clap^{복습}
[klæp]

v. 박수를 치다
When you clap, you hit your hands together to show appreciation or attract attention.

ferocious
[fəróuʃəs]

a. 잔인한, 지독한, 사나운
A ferocious animal, person, or action is very fierce and violent.

weary*
[wíəri]

a. 피로한, 지친 (weariness n. 피로; 지루함)
If you are weary, you are very tired.

intense*
[inténs]

a. 강렬한, 격렬한, 심한
Intense is used to describe something that is very great or extreme in strength or degree.

sigh*
[sai]

v. 한숨 쉬다; n. 한숨, 탄식
When you sigh, you let out a deep breath, as a way of expressing feelings such as disappointment, tiredness, or pleasure.

aloud*
[əláud]

a. 소리 내어, 큰 소리로
When you say something, read, or laugh aloud, you speak or laugh so that other people can hear you.

insistent
[insístənt]

a. 집요한, 고집하는, 강요하는, 우기는
Someone who is insistent keeps insisting that a particular thing should be done or is the case.

tug*
[tʌg]

v. (세게) 당기다, 끌다; 노력[분투]하다; n. 힘껏 당김; 분투, 노력
If you tug something or tug at it, you give it a quick and usually strong pull.

loose**
[lu:s]

a. 풀린, 헐거운, 꽉 죄지 않는
Something that is loose is not firmly held or fixed in place.

thread**
[θred]

n. 실, 바느질 실; vt. 실을 꿰다
A thread is a long very thin piece of a material such as cotton, nylon, or silk, especially one that is used in sewing.

particular^{복습}
[pərtíkjələr]

a. 특정한, 특별한, 특유의
You use particular to emphasize that you are talking about one thing or one kind of thing rather than other similar ones.

perch*
[pə:rtʃ]

v. (높은 곳에) 앉(히)다, 놓다; n. (새의) 횃대; 높은 자리
To perch somewhere means to be on the top or edge of something.

cease^{복습}
[si:s]

v. 그만두다, 중지하다
If you cease something, you stop it happening or working.

mean***
[mi:n]

① a. (meaner–meanest) 비열한; 성질이 나쁜, 심술궂은
② vt. 의미하다, 뜻하다 ③ a. 평균의, 중간의
If you describe a behavior as mean, you are saying that it is very bad and evil.

daze
[deiz]

vt. 멍하게 하다; 눈부시게 하다; n. 멍한 상태; 눈이 부심 (dazed a. 멍한)

If someone is dazed, they are confused and unable to think clearly, often because of shock or a blow to the head.

comfort ^{복습}
[kʌ́mfərt]

n. 마음이 편안함, 안락; 위로, 위안; vt. 위로[위안]하다

If you are doing something in comfort, you are physically relaxed and contented, and are not feeling any pain or other unpleasant sensations.

mock ^{복습}
[mak]

vt. 흉내 내며 놀리다, 조롱하다; n. 조롱, 놀림감; a. 가짜의, 모의의

If someone mocks you, they show or pretend that they think you are foolish or inferior, for example by saying something funny about you, or by imitating your behavior.

constellation ^{복습}
[kanstəléiʃən]

n. [천문] 별자리, 성좌

A constellation is a group of stars which form a pattern and have a name.

1분에 몇 단어를 읽는지 리딩 속도를 측정해보세요.

$$\frac{539 \text{ words}}{\text{reading time ( ) sec}} \times 60 = (\quad) \text{ WPM}$$

Build Your Vocabulary

stare ^{복습}
[stɛər]
v. 응시하다, 뚫어지게 보다
If you stare at someone or something, you look at them for a long time.

fleck
[flek]
n. 반점, 주근깨; 작은 조각, 부스러기
Flecks are small marks on a surface, or objects that look like small marks.

whisper ^{복습}
[hwíspə:r]
v. 속삭이다
When you whisper, you say something very quietly.

crow ^{복습}
[krou]
① n. 까마귀 ② vi. (수탉이) 울다; n. 수탉의 울음소리
A crow is a large black bird which makes a loud, harsh noise.

flap ^{복습}
[flæp]
v. 펄럭이게 하다, 휘날리다, 퍼덕이다; n. 펄럭임, 퍼덕거림
If a bird or insect flaps its wings or if its wings flap, the wings move quickly up and down.

spread ^{복습}
[spred]
v. 펴다, 펼치다, 퍼지다; 뿌리다; n. 퍼짐, 폭, 넓이
If you spread your arms, hands, fingers, or legs, you stretch them out until they are far apart.

weed ^{복습}
[wi:d]
v. 잡초를 없애다; n. 잡초
If you weed an area, you remove the weeds from it.

hoe
[hou]
v. 괭이로 파다[갈다], 제초하다; n. 괭이
If you hoe a field or crop, you use a hoe on the weeds or soil there.

overboard ^{복습}
[óuvərbɔ̀:rd]
ad. 배 밖으로[에]
If you fall overboard, you fall over the side of a boat into the water.

sink ^{복습}
[siŋk]
v. (sank–sunk) 가라앉다, 침몰하다
If something sinks, it disappears below the surface of a mass of water.

opposite ^{**}
[ápəzit]
a. 반대편의, 맞은편의; 정반대의; n. 정반대의 일; ad. 정반대의 위치에
If one thing is opposite another, it is on the other side of a space from it.

dump ^{복습}
[dʌmp]
n. 쓰레기 더미; vt. 내버리다, 쏟아 버리다, 아무렇게나 내려놓다
A dump is a place where rubbish is left, for example on open ground outside a town.

garbage^{복습}
[gárbidʒ]

n. 쓰레기, 찌꺼기
Garbage consists of unwanted things or waste material such as used paper, empty tins and bottles, and waste food.

claw[*]
[klɔː]

n. 발톱, 집게발; v. (손·발톱 따위로) 할퀴다, 긁다
The claws of a bird or animal are the thin, hard, curved nails at the end of its feet.

tap[*]
[tæp]

① v. 가볍게 두드리다; n. 가볍게 두드리기 ② n. 주둥이, (수도 등의) 꼭지
If you tap something, you hit it with a quick light blow or a series of quick light blows.

beak[*]
[biːk]

n. 새의 부리
A bird's beak is the hard curved or pointed part of its mouth.

remind^{**}
[rimáind]

vt. 생각나게 하다, 상기시키다, 일깨우다
If someone reminds you of a fact or event that you already know about, they say something which makes you think about it.

dusk^{복습}
[dʌsk]

n. 땅거미, 황혼, 어스름
Dusk is the time just before night when the daylight has almost gone but when it is not completely dark.

descend^{복습}
[disénd]

v. (어둠·땅거미 등이) 내려앉다, 깔리다; 다가오다, 엄습하다; 내려가다
When night, dusk, or darkness descends, it starts to get dark.

hum[*]
[hʌm]

n. 윙윙 (소리); v. (벌·기계 등이) 윙윙거리다; 콧노래를 부르다
When you hum a tune, you sing it with your lips closed.

bet^{복습}
[bet]

v. 틀림없다, ~라고 확신하다; 걸다, 내기를 하다; n. 내기, 내기돈
You use expressions such as 'I bet', 'I'll bet', and 'you can bet' to indicate that you are sure something is true.

wire^{복습}
[wáiər]

n. 철사, 전선, 케이블; v. 철사로 매다; 전송하다, 전보로 알리다
A wire is a long thin piece of metal that is used to fasten things or to carry electric current.

hollow^{복습}
[hálou]

a. 공허한; 속이 빈; 오목한; n. 구멍, 움푹한 곳; v. 속이 비다
If you describe a statement, situation, or person as hollow, you mean they have no real value, worth, or effectiveness.

nail^{복습}
[neil]

n. 못; 손톱, 발톱; vt. 못을 박다
A nail is a thin piece of metal with one pointed end and one flat end.

rush^{복습}
[rʌʃ]

n. 쇄도, 돌진; v. 돌진하다, 급히 움직이다, 서두르다
If you experience a rush of a feeling, you suddenly experience it very strongly.

relief^{**}
[rilíːf]

n. 안심, 안도
If you feel a sense of relief, you feel happy because something unpleasant has not happened or is no longer happening.

Chapters Seventeen & Eighteen

1. Why did Bryce give Edward to Sarah Ruth?
   A. It was a birthday present for her.
   B. She had a china doll that broke before and Edward replaced it.
   C. Rabbits were Sarah Ruth's favorite animal.
   D. He wanted to keep it for himself but Sarah Ruth asked for it.

2. What did Bryce and Sarah Ruth's house first look like to Edward?
   A. A barn
   B. A tent
   C. A cardboard box
   D. A chicken coop

3. How did Sarah Ruth treat Edward in a way that was new for him?
   A. She didn't want to give him a new name.
   B. She cradled him like a baby.
   C. She held him roughly by the ears.
   D. She cut his fur very short.

4. What did Bryce tell Sarah Ruth while watching the stars?
   A. He told her about the different constellations.
   B. He told her that the stars would always be there for her.
   C. He told her to make a wish on a falling star.
   D. He told her to look for stars that looked like animals.

5. How did the father react to Edward?
   A. He remembered how he had broken the earlier doll and picked
      Edward up carefully.
   B. He handled Edward roughly and said that it didn't matter if
      Sarah Ruth had a doll.
   C. He threatened to break Edward's china head.
   D. He completely ignored Edward and his children.

6. What did Sarah Ruth do while Bryce worked doing the
   day?
   A. She held Edward and played with a box full of buttons.
   B. She read books and drew pictures with Edward.
   C. She cooked food for Bryce and her father.
   D. She tried making new clothes for Edward.

7. How did Bryce surprise Sarah Ruth using Edward?
   A. He used twine to make it look like Edward was dancing.
   B. He used paint to draw on a new face for Edward.
   C. He bought Edward new clean clothes.
   D. He used twine to make a special bed for Edward next to Sarah
      Ruth.

Build Your Vocabulary

sling ^{복습}
[sliŋ]

vt. (slung–slung) 던져 올리다, 걸치다; 투석기로 쏘다
If you sling something over your shoulder or over something such as a chair, you hang it there loosely.

smash[*]
[smæʃ]

v. 때려 부수다, 깨뜨리다; 세게 충돌하다; n. 강타; 부서지는 소리; 분쇄
If you smash something or if it smashes, it breaks into many pieces, for example when it is hit or dropped.

loathe
[louð]

vt. 몹시 싫어하다
If you loathe something or someone, you dislike them very much.

replace ^{복습}
[ripléis]

v. 대신하다, 대체하다 (replacement n. 대체, 교체)
If one thing or person replaces another, the first is used or acts instead of the second.

offend ^{복습}
[əfénd]

v. 불쾌하게 하다, 성나게 하다; 죄를 범하다
If you offend someone, you say or do something rude which upsets or embarrasses them.

admit^{***}
[ædmít]

v. 인정하다
If you admit that something bad, unpleasant, or embarrassing is true, you agree, often unwillingly, that it is true.

prefer ^{복습}
[prifə́ːr]

vt. ~을 좋아하다, 차라리 ~을 택하다 (preferable a. 차라리 나은, 더 좋은)
If you say that one thing is preferable to another, you mean that it is more desirable or suitable.

alternative^{**}
[ɔːltə́ːrnətiv]

n. 대안, 대체수단; 양자택일; a. 하나를 택해야 할, 양자택일의
If one thing is an alternative to another, the first can be found, used, or done instead of the second.

post^{**}
[poust]

① n. 기둥, 말뚝 ② n. 우편, 우체국; vt. 우송하다, 우체통에 넣다
③ n. 수비대, 주둔 부대; 지위; vt. 배치하다
A post is a strong upright pole made of wood or metal that is fixed into the ground.

crooked
[krúkid]

a. 비뚤어진, 구부러진
If you describe something as crooked, especially something that is usually straight, you mean that it is bent or twisted.

coop
[kuːp]

n. 닭장, 우리; v. ~을 가두다
A coop is a cage where you keep small animals or birds such as chickens and rabbits.

86

lay***
[lei]

v. (laid–laid) 놓다, 눕히다; 알을 낳다
If you lay something somewhere, you put it there in a careful, gentle, or neat way.

light^{복습}
[lait]

v. (lit/lighted–lit/lighted) 불을 붙이다, 빛을 비추다; 불이 붙다; n. 빛
If you light something such as a cigarette or fire, or if it lights, it starts burning.

whisper^{복습}
[hwíspə:r]

v. 속삭이다
When you whisper, you say something very quietly.

immediately^{복습}
[imí:diətli]

ad. 곧바로, 즉시
If something happens immediately, it happens without any delay.

cough^{복습}
[kɔ:f]

v. 기침하다; n. 기침
When you cough, you force air out of your throat with a sudden, harsh noise. You often cough when you are ill, or when you are nervous or want to attract someone's attention.

fleck^{복습}
[flek]

n. 반점, 주근깨; 작은 조각, 부스러기 (flecked a. 반점이 있는)
Something that is flecked with something is marked or covered with small bits of it.

oblige*
[əbláidʒ]

vt. (남의) 기대에 부응하다, 베풀다; 의무적으로 ~하게 하다
To oblige someone means to be helpful to them by doing what they have asked you to do.

cabin*
[kǽbin]

n. (통나무) 오두막집; 객실, 선실
A cabin is a small wooden house, especially one in an area of forests or mountains.

cast***
[kæst]

v. (빛을) 발하다; (눈·시선을) 던지다; n. 던지기; 깁스
If something casts a light or shadow somewhere, it causes it to appear there.

tremble*
[trembl]

v. 떨다, 떨리다 (trembling a. 떨리는, 진동하는)
If something trembles, it shakes slightly.

hunch
[hʌntʃ]

v. 둥글게 구부리다; n. 예감, 직감
If you hunch forward, you raise your shoulders, put your head down, and lean forward, often because you are cold, ill, or unhappy.

mournful*
[mɔ́:rnfəl]

a. 슬픔에 잠긴, 슬퍼하는; 애처로운
If you are mournful, you are very sad.

clap^{복습}
[klæp]

v. 박수를 치다
When you clap, you hit your hands together to show appreciation or attract attention.

rarely**
[réərli]

ad. 좀처럼 ~않다, 드물게
If something rarely happens, it does not happen very often.

string^{복습}
[striŋ]

v. (strung–strung) 묶다, 매달다; n. 끈, 실; (악기의) 현[줄]
If you string something somewhere, you hang it up between two or more objects.

limit[**]
[límit]
vt. 제한하다, 한정하다; n. 제한, 한계
If you limit yourself to something, or if someone or something limits you, the number of things that you have or do is reduced.

provoke[*]
[prəvóuk]
vt. 일으키다, 유발시키다; 화나게 하다, 도발하다
If something provokes a reaction, it causes the reaction.

fit[복습]
[fit]
① n. 발작, 경련 ② v. 꼭 맞다, 어울리다; a. 적합한, 알맞은
If you have a fit of coughing or laughter, you suddenly start coughing or laughing in an uncontrollable way.

curl[복습]
[kə:rl]
v. 몸을 웅크리다; 감(기)다; 곱슬하다; n. 곱슬머리, 동그랗게 말리는 것
(uncurl v. 똑바로 펴다)
To uncurl means to move or cause to move out of a curled or rolled up position.

rock[**]
[rak]
① v. 앞뒤[좌우]로 흔들(리)다; 동요하다 ② n. 암석, 바위; [음악] 록
When something rocks or when you rock it, it moves slowly and regularly backward and forward or from side to side.

cradle[*]
[kreidl]
v. (안전하게 보호하듯이) 떠받치다, 살짝 안다; n. 유아용 침대; (전화의) 수화기대
If you cradle someone or something in your arms or hands, you hold them carefully and gently.

singular[직습]
[síŋgjulər]
a. 기묘한, 이상한; 뛰어난, 보기 드문; 유일한, 단독의
If you describe someone or something as singular, you mean that they are strange or unusual.

sensation[*]
[senséiʃən]
n. 감각, 느낌, 기분
A sensation is a physical feeling.

fierce[복습]
[fiərs]
a. 격렬한, 지독한; 사나운 (fiercely ad. 맹렬히, 사납게)
Fierce feelings or actions are very intense or enthusiastic, or involve great activity.

flood[**]
[flʌd]
v. 쇄도하다, 물밀듯이 밀려들다; 넘치다, 범람하다; n. 홍수; 쇄도, 폭주
If an emotion, feeling, or thought floods you, you suddenly feel it very intensely.

pat[*]
[pæt]
v. 톡톡 가볍게 치다, (애정을 담아) 쓰다듬다; n. 쓰다듬기
If you pat something or someone, you tap them lightly, usually with your hand held flat.

hush[*]
[hʌʃ]
v. 쉿, 조용히 해[울지 마]; ~을 조용히 시키다; n. 침묵, 고요
You say 'Hush!' to someone when you are asking or telling them to be quiet.

murmur[*]
[mə́:rmə:r]
v. 중얼거리다; 투덜거리다; n. 중얼거림
If you murmur something, you say it very quietly, so that not many people can hear what you are saying.

crack[복습]
[kræk]
v. 날카로운 소리를 내다; 깨(지)다, 금이 가다; n. 갈라진 금; 갑작스런 날카로운 소리
If something cracks, or if you crack it, it makes a sharp sound like the sound of a piece of wood breaking.

tin[복습]
[tin]
n. 주석, 양철 깡통[냄비]
Tin is a soft silvery-white metal.

1분에 몇 단어를 읽는지 리딩 속도를 측정해보세요.

$$\frac{814 \text{ words}}{\text{reading time (\quad) sec}} \times 60 = (\quad) \text{ WPM}$$

Build Your Vocabulary

cough ^{복습}
[kɔːf]

v. 기침하다; n. 기침
When you cough, you force air out of your throat with a sudden, harsh noise. You often cough when you are ill, or when you are nervous or want to attract someone's attention.

frighten^{**}
[fraitn]

v. 놀라게 하다, 섬뜩하게 하다; 기겁하다 (frightened a. 겁먹은, 무서워하는)
If something or someone frightens you, they cause you to suddenly feel afraid, anxious, or nervous.

crush^{**}
[krʌʃ]

v. 짓밟다; 부서지다; (정신·희망을) 꺾다; n. 눌러 터뜨림
To crush something means to press it very hard so that its shape is destroyed or so that it breaks into pieces.

sass
[sæs]

v. (남에게) 건방진 대꾸[행동]를 하다; n. 건방진 말대꾸[행동]
To sass means to talk or answer back in an insolent manner.

slap[*]
[slæp]

v. 찰싹 때리다, 탁 놓다; n. 찰싹 (때림)
If you slap someone, you hit them with the palm of your hand.

bully[*]
[búli]

n. 약자를 괴롭히는 사람; v. 괴롭히다, 겁주다
A bully is someone who uses their strength or power to hurt or frighten other people.

hardly^{***}
[háːrdli]

ad. 조금도[전혀] ~아니다[않다]
You use hardly in expressions such as hardly ever, hardly any, and hardly anyone to mean almost never, almost none, or almost no-one.

fortunately^{복습}
[fɔ́ːrtʃənətli]

ad. 다행히도, 운좋게도
Fortunately is used to introduce or indicate a statement about an event or situation that is good.

lap^{복습}
[læp]

① n. 무릎; (트랙의) 한 바퀴 ② v. (파도가) 찰싹거리다, (할짝할짝) 핥다
If you have something on your lap, it is on top of your legs and near to your body.

arrange^{복습}
[əréindʒ]

v. 가지런히 하다, 배열하다; 준비하다
If you arrange things somewhere, you place them in a particular position, usually in order to make them look attractive or tidy.

fit^{복습}
[fit]

① n. 발작, 경련 ② v. 꼭 맞다, 어울리다; a. 적합한, 알맞은
If you have a fit of coughing or laughter, you suddenly start coughing or laughing in an uncontrollable way.

particular^{복습}
[pərtíkjələr]

a. 특정한, 특별한, 특유의 (particularly ad. 특히)
You use particularly to indicate that what you are saying applies especially to one thing or situation.

squeeze*
[skwi:z]

vt. 꽉 쥐다[죄다], 압착하다; n. 압착, 짜냄; 꽉 끌어 안음
If you squeeze something, you press it firmly, usually with your hands.

suck^{복습}
[sʌk]

v. 빨다, 흡수하다; 삼키다; n. 빨아들임
If something sucks a liquid, gas, or object in a particular direction, it draws it there with a powerful force.

intrusive
[intrú:siv]

a. 거슬리는; 참견하는, 방해하는
Something that is intrusive disturbs your mood or your life in a way you do not like.

clingy
[klíŋi]

a. (= clinging) 남에게 의존하는, 잘 들러붙는; 몸에 꼭 맞는
If you describe someone as clingy, you mean that they become very attached to people and depend on them too much.

sort***
[sɔ:rt]

n. 종류, 부류; vt. 분류하다, 골라내다
If you talk about a particular sort of something, you are talking about a class of things that have particular features in common and that belong to a larger group of related things.

annoy**
[ənɔ́i]

v. 성가시게 굴다, 괴롭히다; 불쾌하다
If someone or something annoys you, it makes you fairly angry and impatient.

protect^{복습}
[prətékt]

v. 보호하다, 막다, 지키다
To protect someone or something means to prevent them from being harmed or damaged.

biscuit**
[bískit]

n. 비스킷
A biscuit is a small flat cake that is crisp and usually sweet.

twine
[twain]

n. 꼰 실, 삼끈, 꼬기, 감김; 엉클어짐, 뒤얽힘; v. 감다, 꼬다
Twine is strong string used especially in gardening and farming.

tentative*
[téntətiv]

a. 머뭇거리는, 주저하는; 잠정적인, 임시의
If someone is tentative, they are cautious and not very confident because they are uncertain or afraid.

sway*
[swei]

v. 흔들(리)다, 동요하다; 설득하다; n. 동요
When people or things sway, they lean or swing slowly from one side to the other.

lively*
[láivli]

a. 활기찬, 생기에 넘치는, 기운찬
You can describe someone as lively when they behave in an enthusiastic and cheerful way.

tune*
[tju:n]

n. 곡조, 선율; v. 조율하다, 조정하다
A tune is a series of musical notes that is pleasant and easy to remember.

lay^{복습}
[lei]

v. (laid-laid) 놓다, 눕히다; 알을 낳다
If you lay something somewhere, you put it there in a careful, gentle, or neat way.

rock^{복습}
[rak]

① v. 앞뒤[좌우]로 흔들(리)다; 동요하다 ② n. 암석, 바위; [음악] 록
When something rocks or when you rock it, it moves slowly and regularly backward and forward or from side to side.

rub^{복습}
[rʌb]

v. 쓰다듬다; 문지르다, 맞비비다; 닦다, 윤내다; n. 닦기, 마찰
If you rub a part of your body, you move your hand or fingers backward and forward over it while pressing firmly.

nasty[*]
[nǽsti]

a. 좋지 않은, 추잡한, 더러운; 못된, 고약한
Something that is nasty is very unpleasant to see, experience, or feel.

lie^{복습}
[lai]

vi. (lay-lain) 눕다, 누워 있다; 놓여 있다, 위치하다
If you are lying somewhere, you are in a horizontal position and are not standing or sitting.

stare^{복습}
[stɛər]

v. 응시하다, 똑바로게 보다
If you stare at someone or something, you look at them for a long time.

stain^{복습}
[stein]

v. 더러워지다, 얼룩지게 하다; n. 얼룩, 오점 (stained a. 얼룩투성이의)
If a liquid stains something, the thing becomes coloured or marked by the liquid.

streak[*]
[striːk]

v. 질주하다; 줄을 긋다; n. 경향, 기미; 줄
If something or someone streaks somewhere, they move there very quickly.

1. How did Sarah Ruth's condition change after Edward arrived?
   A. Her coughing decreased and she was eventually cured.
   B. Her coughing increased and she steadily got worse.
   C. She stayed mostly the same.
   D. She got better for a little but then suddenly got sick again.

2. Where was Edward when Sarah Ruth stopped breathing and why was he there?
   A. Edward was on the floor because Sarah Ruth had dropped him.
   B. Edward was in Sarah Ruth's arms because he comforted her.
   C. Edward was at the head of the bed because he was placed there to watch her.
   D. Edward was placed in a chair because Bryce was holding Sarah Ruth.

3. What did the father decide to do that upset Bryce?
   A. He wanted to take Edward away and sell him.
   B. He told Bryce that he should have been a better brother.
   C. He said he loved her and took her to be buried.
   D. He didn't do anything about Sarah Ruth and just left Bryce with her.

4. Why did Bryce decide to take Edward to Memphis?

    A. He wanted to meet his relatives who lived there.

    B. He wanted to take him to a doll collector and earn some money.

    C. He wanted to go to music school to become a famous musician.

    D. He wanted to use Edward for a show on the streets.

5. What did the mother say when her child wanted to touch Edward?

    A. She called Edward dirty and nasty.

    B. She called Edward sad and pitiful.

    C. She said that she would buy the child a rabbit doll.

    D. She said that it wasn't a real rabbit.

6. What did Bryce start to do while playing the harmonica and making Edward dance?

    A. He started to dance too.

    B. He started to tap his foot on the pavement.

    C. He started to hold the box out for money.

    D. He started to cry.

7. How did Edward feel when he saw Pellegrina in the crowd?

    A. He wanted her to know that he missed Abilene.

    B. He wanted her to know that he hated her.

    C. He wanted her to know that he had learned to love.

    D. He wanted her to tell him the story of the princess again.

1분에 몇 단어를 읽는지 리딩 속도를 측정해보세요.

$$\frac{422 \ words}{reading \ time \ (\qquad) \ sec} \times 60 = (\qquad) \ WPM$$

Build Your Vocabulary

soggy
[sági]
a. 물에 잠긴, 함빡 젖은
Something that is soggy is unpleasantly wet.

unravel
[ʌnrǽvəl]
v. (실 등을) 풀다; 해명하다, 해결하다
If you unravel something that is knotted, woven, or knitted, or if it unravels, it becomes one straight piece again or separates into its different threads.

twine^{복습}
[twain]
n. 꼰 실, 삼끈; 꼬기, 감김; 엉클어짐, 뒤얽힘; v. 감다, 꼬다
Twine is strong string used especially in gardening and farming.

refuse***
[rifjú:z]
vt. 거절하다, 거부하다
If you refuse to do something, you deliberately do not do it, or you say firmly that you will not do it.

cough^{복습}
[kɔ:f]
v. 기침하다; n. 기침
When you cough, you force air out of your throat with a sudden, harsh noise. You often cough when you are ill, or when you are nervous or want to attract someone's attention.

ragged*
[rǽgid]
a. (솜씨·호흡 등이) 고르지 못한, 거친; (옷 등이) 찢어진, 해진; 남루한, 초라한
You can say that something is ragged when it is untidy or uneven.

well***
[wel]
① n. 우물 모양의 구멍, 움푹한 곳, 우물; v. 솟아 나오다, 내뿜다, 분출하다
② ad. 잘, 좋게
A well is a hole in the ground from which a supply of water is extracted.

lap^{복습}
[læp]
① n. 무릎; (트랙의) 한 바퀴 ② v. (파도가) 찰싹거리다, (할짝할짝) 핥다
If you have something on your lap, it is on top of your legs and near to your body.

rock^{복습}
[rak]
① v. 앞뒤[좌우]로 흔들(리)다; 동요하다 ② n. 암석, 바위; [음악] 록
When something rocks or when you rock it, it moves slowly and regularly backward and forward or from side to side.

weep*
[wi:p]
v. (wept-wept) 눈물을 흘리다, 울다; 물기를 내뿜다
If someone weeps, they cry.

wonder^{복습}
[wʌ́ndə:r]
v. 이상하게 여기다, 호기심을 가지다; n. 경탄할 만한 것, 경이
If you wonder about something, you think about it because it interests you and you want to know more about it.

bear 복습
[bɛər]

① v. 견디다; (의무·책임을) 지다; 낳다 ② n. 곰
If you bear an unpleasant experience, you accept it because you are unable to do anything about it.

yell*
[jel]

v. 소리치다, 고함치다; n. 고함소리, 부르짖음
If you yell, you shout loudly, usually because you are excited, angry, or in pain.

insist**
[insíst]

v. 주장하다, 우기다
If you insist that something is the case, you say so very firmly and refuse to say otherwise, even though other people do not believe you.

bury 복습
[béri]

vt. 묻다, 파묻다, 매장하다
To bury something means to put it into a hole in the ground and cover it up with earth.

prevail*
[privéil]

vi. 우세하다; 유행하다, 널리 보급되다
If one side in a battle, contest, or dispute prevails, it wins.

blanket 복습
[blǽŋkit]

n. 담요, 모포; v. ~을 (담요로 덮듯이) 전면을 덮다; 담요로 덮다[싸다]
A blanket is a large square or rectangular piece of thick cloth, especially one which you put on a bed to keep you warm.

mutter*
[mʌ́tər]

v. 중얼거리다, 불평하다; n. 중얼거림, 불평
If you mutter, you speak very quietly so that you cannot easily be heard, often because you are complaining about something.

1분에 몇 단어를 읽는지 리딩 속도를 측정해보세요.

$$\frac{546 \text{ words}}{\text{reading time ( ) sec}} \times 60 = (\qquad) \text{ WPM}$$

Build Your Vocabulary

folk^{복습}
[fouk]

n. (pl.) (일반적인) 사람들: 가족, 부모
You can refer to people as folk or folks.

scarecrow^{**}
[skέərkròu]

n. 허수아비
A scarecrow is an object in the shape of a person, which is put in a field where crops are growing in order to frighten birds away.

hang^{복습}
[hæŋ]

v. 매달리다, 달려 있다; 걸다, 달아매다; 배회하다; 교수형에 처하다
If something hangs in a high place or position, or if you hang it there, it is attached there so it does not touch the ground.

hollow^{복습}
[hálou]

a. 공허한, 속이 빈, 오목한; n. 구멍; 움푹한 곳; v. 속이 비다
If you describe a statement, situation, or person as hollow, you mean they have no real value, worth, or effectiveness.

ache^{복습}
[eik]

vi. 쑤시다, 아프다; n. 아픔, 쑤심
If you ache or a part of your body aches, you feel a steady, fairly strong pain.

string^{복습}
[striŋ]

n. 끈, 실; (악기의) 현(줄); v. 묶다, 매달다
String is thin rope made of twisted threads, used for tying things together or tying up parcels.

bow^{복습}
[bau]

① v. 머리를 숙이다, 굽히다 ② n. 활; 곡선
When you bow, you move your head or the top half of your body forward and downward as a formal way of greeting them or showing respect.

shuffle
[ʃʌfl]

v. (댄스에서) 발을 끌며 짧은 스텝으로 추다; 질질 끌다, 발을 끌며 걷다
If you shuffle somewhere, you walk there without lifting your feet properly off the ground.

sway^{복습}
[swei]

v. 흔들(리)다, 동요하다; 설득하다; n. 동요
When people or things sway, they lean or swing slowly from one side to the other.

stare^{복습}
[stɛər]

v. 응시하다, 뚫어지게 보다
If you stare at someone or something, you look at them for a long time.

lid[*]
[lid]

n. 뚜껑
A lid is the top of a box or other container which can be removed or raised when you want to open the container.

96

encourage[**] vt. 용기를 북돋우다, 장려하다
[inkə́:ridʒ]
If you encourage someone, you give them confidence, hope, or support.

change[***] ① n. 거스름돈, 잔돈; v. 잔돈으로 바꾸다 ② v. 변하다, 바꾸다; n. 변화, 변경
[tʃeindʒ]
Change is coins, rather than paper money.

nasty[복습] a. 더러운, 추잡한, 좋지 않은; 못된, 고약한
[nǽsti]
If you describe something as nasty, you mean it is unattractive, undesirable, or in bad taste.

sin[**] n. 죄, 죄악
[sin]
A sin is any action or behavior that people disapprove of or consider morally wrong.

pause[복습] n. 멈춤, 중지; vi. 중단하다, 잠시 멈추다
[pɔːz]
A pause is a short period when you stop doing something before continuing.

particular[복습] a. 특정한, 특별한, 특유의
[pərtíkjələr]
You use particular to emphasize that you are talking about one thing or one kind of thing rather than other similar ones.

lengthen[*] v. 길어지다, 늘어나다; 길게 하다, 늘이다
[léŋkθən]
When something lengthens or when you lengthen it, it increases in length.

dust[복습] n. 먼지, 티끌; v. 먼지를 털다[닦다] (dusty a. 먼지투성이의)
[dʌst]
If a room, house, or object is dusty, it is covered with very small pieces of dirt.

pavement[*] n. 포장 도로
[péivmənt]
The pavement is the hard surface of a road.

lean[복습] ① v. 기대다, 의지하다; 기울다, 기대어 세우다; 상체를 굽히다 ② a. 야윈, 마른
[liːn]
If you lean on or against someone or something, you rest against them so that they partly support your weight.

cane[*] n. 지팡이
[kein]
A cane is a long thin stick with a curved or round top which you can use to support yourself when you are walking.

nod[복습] v. 끄덕이다, 끄덕여 표시하다; n. (동의·인사·신호·명령의) 끄덕임
[nad]
If you nod, you move your head downward and upward to show agreement, understanding, or approval.

jerk[*] ① v. 갑자기 움직이다; n. 갑자기 움직임; 반사 운동 ② n. 바보, 멍청이
[dʒəːrk]
If you jerk something or someone in a particular direction, or they jerk in a particular direction, they move a short distance very suddenly and quickly.

hobble vi. 절뚝거리며 걷다
[habl]
If you hobble, you walk in an awkward way with small steps, for example because your foot is injured.

Chapters Twenty-One & Twenty-Two

1. Where did Bryce take Edward after playing on the street?
   A. A diner named Neal's
   B. A restaurant named Marlene's
   C. A grocery store named Ned's
   D. A doll shop named Nick's

2. How did Edward feel about being pushed around by Marlene?
   A. He felt annoyed that a famous rabbit like himself would be treated like that.
   B. He felt broken and didn't really mind it at all.
   C. He felt happy that people still touched him even though he was dirty.
   D. He felt sad because she reminded him of Sarah Ruth.

3. How did Neal react to Bryce not having money and making Edward dance instead?
   A. Neal thought that it was funny and let Bryce eat for free.
   B. Neal liked Edward and wanted to take Edward for the cost of the meal.
   C. Neal felt sorry for Bryce and let him work for him to pay for the meal.
   D. Neal was angry and broke Edward's head on the counter.

4. How did Edward get to the home on Egypt Street?
   A. He rode on Lucy's back.
   B. He was carried by Abilene.
   C. He walked there on his own.
   D. He used his wings to fly there.

5. Which of the following people were NOT waiting for Edward inside the house?
   A. Bull and Lucy
   B. Abilene
   C. Nellie and Lawrence
   D. Bryce and Sarah

6. Why was Sarah Ruth not with the others in the house?
   A. She was a constellation in the night sky.
   B. She was waiting outside on the lawn for him.
   C. She was making a wish outside on a falling star.
   D. She was still in her bed at her own home.

7. Why did everyone stop Edward from flying away?
   A. They were afraid that Edward would hurt himself.
   B. They wanted Edward to stay with them.
   C. They told Edward that Sarah Ruth would come to them later.
   D. They wanted to give Edward a message for Sarah Ruth first.

1분에 몇 단어를 읽는지 리딩 속도를 측정해보세요.

$$\frac{664 \text{ words}}{\text{reading time (\quad) sec}} \times 60 = (\qquad) \text{ WPM}$$

Build Your Vocabulary

diner
[dáinər]
n. 간이 식당; 식사하는 사람
A diner is a small cheap restaurant that is open all day.

flash^{**}
[flæʃ]
v. 번쩍이다, 빛나다; n. 섬광, 번쩍임
If a light flashes or if you flash a light, it shines with a sudden bright light, especially as quick, regular flashes of light.

stool[*]
[stu:l]
n. (등이 없는) 걸상; 발판
A stool is a seat with legs but no support for your arms or back.

lean^{복습}
[li:n]
① v. 기대어 세우다, 기울이다; 상체를 굽히다; 기대다, 의지하다 ② a. 야윈, 마른
If you lean an object on or against something, you place the object so that it is partly supported by that thing.

forehead[*]
[fɔ́:rhèd]
n. 이마
Your forehead is the area at the front of your head between your eyebrows and your hair.

waitress
[wéitris]
n. 여종업원
A waitress is a woman who works in a restaurant, serving people with food and drink.

reckon^{복습}
[rékən]
vt. ~라고 생각하다; 세다, 계산하다
If you reckon that something is true, you think that it is true.

tuck[*]
[tʌk]
v. 밀어 넣다, 쑤셔 넣다; n. 접어 넣은 단
If you tuck something somewhere, you put it there so that it is safe, comfortable, or neat.

check^{**}
[tʃek]
n. 계산서; 수표; 검사, 점검
The check in a restaurant is a piece of paper on which the price of your meal is written and which you are given before you pay.

spatula
[spǽtʃulə]
n. 주걱
A spatula is an object like a knife with a wide, flat blade.

thwack
[θwæk]
n. 찰싹 때리는 소리; vt. 찰싹 때리다
A thwack is a sound made when two solid objects hit each other hard.

serve^{복습}
[sə:rv]
v. 식사 시중을 들다, (음식을) 제공하다; (사람·조직·국가 등을 위해) 일하다, 복무하다; n. (테니스 등의) 서브
When you serve food and drink, you give people food and drink.

100

throat ^{복습}
[θrout]

n. 목, 목구멍; 좁은 통로 (clear one's throat idiom 목을 가다듬다, 헛기침하다)
Your throat is the back of your mouth and the top part of the tubes that go down into your stomach and your lungs.

tap ^{복습}
[tæp]

① v. 가볍게 두드리다; n. 가볍게 두드리기 ② n. 주둥이, (수도 등의) 꼭지
If you tap something, you hit it with a quick light blow or a series of quick light blows.

string ^{복습}
[striŋ]

n. 끈, 실; (악기의) 현[줄]; v. 묶다, 매달다
String is thin rope made of twisted threads, used for tying things together or tying up parcels.

attach ^{복습}
[ətǽtʃ]

vt. 붙이다, 달다 (attached a. 붙어진)
If you attach something to an object, you connect it or fasten it to the object.

shuffle ^{복습}
[ʃʌfl]

v. (댄스에서) 발을 끌며 짧은 스텝으로 추다; 질질 끌다, 발을 끌며 걷다
If you shuffle somewhere, you walk there without lifting your feet properly off the ground.

warn ^{***}
[wɔːrn]

v. 경고하다; ~에게 통지[통고]하다
If you warn someone about something such as a possible danger or problem, you tell them about it so that they are aware of it.

grab ^{복습}
[græb]

v. 부여잡다, 움켜쥐다; n. 부여잡기
If you grab something, you take it or pick it up suddenly and roughly.

swing ^{복습}
[swiŋ]

v. (swung-swung) 휘두르다, (한 점을 축으로 하여) 빙 돌다, 휙 움직이다
If you swing something, you try to move it in a curve or arc, usually with the intent of hitting.

edge ^{**}
[edʒ]

n. 끝, 가장자리, 모서리
The edge of something is the place or line where it stops, or the part of it that is furthest from the middle.

crack ^{복습}
[kræk]

n. 갑작스런 날카로운 소리; 갈라진 금; v. 금이 가다, 깨(지)다; 날카로운 소리를 내다
A crack is a sharp sound, like the sound of a piece of wood breaking.

1분에 몇 단어를 읽는지 리딩 속도를 측정해보세요.

$$\frac{501 \text{ words}}{\text{reading time (} \quad \text{) sec}} \times 60 = (\quad) \text{ WPM}$$

Build Your Vocabulary

dusk^{복습}
[dʌsk]

n. 땅거미, 황혼, 어스름
Dusk is the time just before night when the daylight has almost gone but when it is not completely dark.

sidewalk[*]
[sáidwɔːk]

n. (포장한) 보도, 인도
A sidewalk is a path with a hard surface by the side of a road.

assistance^{**}
[əsístəns]

n. 도움, 조력, 원조
If you give someone assistance, you help them do a job or task by doing part of the work for them.

lead^{복습}
[liːd]

① vt. (led–led) 인도하다, 이끌다, 인솔하다; n. 선도, 솔선, 지휘
② n. [광물] 납
If a road, gate, or door leads somewhere, you can get there by following the road or going through the gate or door.

wag^{복습}
[wæg]

v. (꼬리 등을) 흔들다, 흔들리다; n. 흔들기
When a dog wags its tail, it repeatedly waves its tail from side to side.

gruff
[grʌf]

a. (목소리가) 거친, 쉰; 퉁명스러운
A gruff voice sounds low and rough.

nod^{복습}
[nad]

v. 끄덕이다, 끄덕여 표시하다; n. (동의·인사·신호·명령의) 끄덕임
If you nod, you move your head downward and upward to show agreement, understanding, or approval.

constellation^{복습}
[kanstəléiʃən]

n. [천문] 별자리, 성좌
A constellation is a group of stars which form a pattern and have a name.

pang[*]
[pæŋ]

n. 비통, 상심; 격통, 고통
A pang is a sudden strong feeling or emotion, for example of sadness or pain.

sorrow^{***}
[sárou]

n. 슬픔, 비통; 후회
Sorrow is a feeling of deep sadness or regret.

familiar^{***}
[fəmíljər]

a. 친숙한, 잘 알고 있는; 친한; 잘 알려진
If someone or something is familiar to you, you recognize them or know them well.

flutter^{**}
[flʌ́tər]

v. 펄럭이다, 흔들다; (새 등이) 파닥이다, 날갯짓하다; n. 펄럭임
If something thin or light flutters, or if you flutter it, it moves up and down or from side to side with a lot of quick, light movements.

magnificent[**]
[mægnífəsnt]

a. 웅장한, 잔연한, 훌륭한
If you say that something or someone is magnificent, you mean that you think they are extremely good, beautiful, or impressive.

elegant[복습]
[éligənt]

a. 품위 있는, 우아한, 고상한
If you describe a person or thing as elegant, you mean that they are pleasing and graceful in appearance or style.

soar[*]
[sɔːr]

vi. 높이 치솟다, 날아오르다; n. 높이 날기, 비상
If your spirits soar, you suddenly start to feel very happy.

spread[복습]
[spred]

v. 퍼지다, 펴다, 펼치다; 뿌리다; n. 퍼짐, 폭, 넓이
If you spread your arms, hands, fingers, or legs, you stretch them out until they are far apart.

terrific[*]
[tərífik]

a. 굉장한, 엄청난; 대단한, 멋진
Terrific means very great in amount, degree, or intensity.

lunge
[lʌndʒ]

n. 돌입, 돌진; v. 돌진하다
Lunge means the act of moving forward suddenly and clumsily.

grab[복습]
[græb]

v. 부여잡다, 움켜쥐다; n. 부여잡기
If you grab something, you take it or pick it up suddenly and roughly.

wrestle[*]
[resl]

v. 씨름하다, 레슬링하다, 맞붙어 싸우다; n. 맞붙어 싸움; 분투, 고투
If you wrestle a person or thing somewhere, you move them there using a lot of force, for example by twisting a part of someone's body into a painful position.

beat[복습]
[biːt]

v. (beat-beaten) (날개를) 퍼덕거리다; 치다, 두들기다; (심장이) 고동치다; n. [음악] 박자, 고동
When a bird or insect beats its wings or when its wings beat, its wings move up and down.

firm[복습]
[fəːrm]

① a. 굳은, 단단한; 견고한 (firmly ad. 굳게) ② n. 회사
If you describe someone as firm, you mean they behave in a way that shows that they are not going to change their mind, or that they are the person who is in control.

stand[***]
[stænd]

vi. 참다, 견디다; 서다, 일어서다; n. 가판대, 좌판; 관람석
If you cannot stand something, you cannot bear it or tolerate it.

lick[**]
[lik]

vt. 핥다; (불길이 허처럼) 날름거리다; 넘실거리다; n. 핥기
When people or animals lick something, they move their tongue across its surface.

Chapters Twenty-Three & Twenty-Four

1. The doll mender said that Edward's head broke, but what did Edward say was broken?
   A. His mind
   B. His heart
   C. His body
   D. His dreams

2. How did Edward appear when he woke up?
   A. He was wearing a red suit.
   B. He was sitting on a doll shelf.
   C. He had new wings.
   D. He was naked on a wooden table.

3. Why was Bryce able to get Edward fixed?
   A. Bryce gave Lucius Clarke the money to fix him.
   B. Lucius Clarke was Bryce's uncle and owed him a favor.
   C. Lucius Clarke would fix Edward but then keep him as his own.
   D. Bryce said that he would just go fix it himself, but Lucius Clarke offered to do it.

4. What did Lucius Clarke plan to do with Edward?
   A. He planned to fix him up and give Edward to his daughter.
   B. He planned to fix him up and sell him in his store.
   C. He planned to fix him up and then give him back to Bryce.
   D. He planned to fix him up and donate him to a museum.

5. Why did Bryce come back to the doll shop?
    A. Bryce wanted to see Edward fixed again one last time.
    B. Bryce came to pick up Edward and bring him home.
    C. Bryce came to ask for a job at the doll shop.
    D. Bryce came to buy Edward back for his street performance.

6. How did Lucius Clarke treat Bryce?
    A. Lucius Clarke was nice and let Bryce hold Edward.
    B. Lucius Clarke was generous and gave Edward to Bryce.
    C. Lucius Clarke was annoyed and told Bryce to never come back again.
    D. Lucius Clarke was disrespectful and called Bryce dirty.

7. How did Lucius Clarke describe Bryce to Edward?
    A. He described Bryce as Edward's young friend with the running nose.
    B. He described Bryce as Edward's young friend with the harmonica.
    C. He described Bryce as Edward's young friend with the gold speckled eyes.
    D. He described Bryce as Edward's young friend with the blond hair.

1분에 몇 단어를 읽는지 리딩 속도를 측정해보세요.

$$\frac{614 \text{ words}}{\text{reading time (\quad) sec}} \times 60 = (\quad) \text{ WPM}$$

Build Your Vocabulary

exceedingly
[iksí:diŋli]

ad. 극도로, 대단히
Exceedingly means very or very much.

cloth**
[klɔ:θ]

n. 옷감, 직물
Cloth is fabric which is made by weaving or knitting a substance such as cotton, wool, silk, or nylon.

surpassing
[sərpǽsiŋ]

a. 뛰어난, 출중한; 놀라운, 탁월한 (surpassingly ad. 뛰어나게, 빼어나게)
That something is surpassing means it is extraordinary, exceeding usual limits especially in excellence.

nonetheless*
[nʌnðəlés]

ad. 그럼에도 불구하고, 그래도, 역시
You use nonetheless when saying something that contrasts with what has just been said.

deal**
[di:l]

v. (dealt–dealt) 다루다, 처리하다; 대우하다, 상대하다; 거래하다; n. 대우; 거래
If you deal with something, you solve a problem or carry out a task.

literal**
[lítərəl]

a. 글자 그대로의; 문자의 (literally ad. 글자 뜻대로, 말 그대로, 정말로)
If you describe something as the literal truth or a literal fact, you are emphasizing that it is true.

mender
[méndər]

n. 고치는 사람, 수선자
A mender is one who repairs something broken or not working.

upset**
[ʌpsét]

v. 당황하게 하다; 뒤엎다; (계획 등을) 망쳐놓다
If something upsets you, it makes you feel worried or unhappy.

head-on
[héd-ón]

ad. 정면으로, 똑바로
If two vehicles hit each other head-on, they hit each other with their fronts pointing towards each other.

pun
[pʌn]

n. 말장난, 신소리; v. 말장난하다, 빗대어 말하다
A pun is a clever and amusing use of a word or phrase with two meanings, or of words with the same sound but different meanings.

intend***
[inténd]

v. 의도하다, ~할 작정이다, ~하려고 생각하다
If you intend to do something, you have decided or planned to do it.

mindless
[máindlis]

a. 신경을 쓰지 않는; 무심한, 어리석은 (mindlessly ad. 의식없이, 분별없이)
If you describe an activity as mindless, you mean that it is so dull that people do it or take part in it without thinking.

modesty[*]
[mádisti]

n. 겸손, 정숙
Someone who shows modesty does not talk much about their abilities or achievements.

aside[복습]
[əsáid]

ad. 한쪽으로; (길을) 비켜
If you take or draw someone aside, you take them a little way away from a group of people in order to talk to them in private.

admit[복습]
[ædmít]

v. 인정하다
If you admit that something bad, unpleasant, or embarrassing is true, you agree, often unwillingly, that it is true.

rescue[**]
[réskju:]

vt. 구조하다, 구출하다; n. 구출, 구원
If you rescue someone, you get them out of a dangerous or unpleasant situation.

whole[***]
[houl]

a. 상처가 없는, 손상되지 않은; 완전한, 전부의
If something is whole, it is in one piece and is not broken or damaged.

brink[*]
[briŋk]

n. (상황이 발생하기) 직전; (벼랑·강가 등의) 끝
If you are on the brink of something, usually something important, terrible, or exciting, you are just about to do it or experience it.

oblivion
[əblíviən]

n. 망각, 잊혀짐, 잊기 쉬움, 건망
Oblivion is the state of having been forgotten or of no longer being considered important.

humble[*]
[hʌmbl]

a. 변변치 않은, 초라한; 겸손한; vt. (교만·권위·의지 등을) 꺾다
A humble person is not proud and does not believe that they are better than other people.

servant[***]
[sə́:rvənt]

n. 하인, 종; 부하
A servant is someone who is employed to work at another person's home.

bow[복습]
[bau]

① v. 머리를 숙이다, 굽히다 ② n. 활; 곡선
When you bow, you move your head or the top half of your body forward and downward as a formal way of greeting them or showing respect.

lie[복습]
[lai]

vi. (lay–lain) 눕다, 누워 있다; 놓여 있다, 위치하다
If you are lying somewhere, you are in a horizontal position and are not standing or sitting.

absorb[**]
[æbsɔ́:rb]

vt. 받아들이다, 흡수하다; 열중시키다
If you absorb information, you learn and understand it.

apparent[복습]
[əpǽrənt]

a. 또렷한, 명백한; 외관상의 (apparently ad. 보아하니, 명백히)
If something is apparent to you, it is clear and obvious to you.

naked[복습]
[néikid]

a. 나체의, 발가벗은; 적나라한
Someone who is naked is not wearing any clothes.

diner[복습]
[dáinər]

n. 간이 식당; 식사하는 사람
A diner is a small cheap restaurant that is open all day.

wonder ^{복습}
[wʌ́ndər]

v. 이상하게 여기다, 호기심을 가지다; n. 경탄할 만한 것, 경이
If you wonder about something, you think about it because it interests you and you want to know more about it.

weep ^{복습}
[wi:p]

v. 눈물을 흘리다, 울다; 물기를 내뿜다
If someone weeps, they cry.

beg***
[beg]

vt. 부탁[간청]하다; 구걸하다, 빌다
If you beg someone to do something, you ask them very anxiously or eagerly to do it.

assistance ^{복습}
[əsístəns]

n. 도움, 조력, 원조
If you give someone assistance, you help them do a job or task by doing part of the work for them.

option**
[ápʃən]

n. 선택(권); v. ~의 선택권을 얻다
An option is something that you can choose to do in preference to one or more alternatives.

considerable**
[kənsídərəbl]

a. 상당한, 꽤 많은; 다수[다량]의; 중요한
Considerable means great in amount or degree.

ability ^{복습}
[əbíləti]

n. 능력, 재능
Your ability to do something is the fact that you can do it.

heal*
[hi:l]

v. (상처·아픔·고장 등을) 낫게 하다, 치료하다
When something heals it, it becomes healthy and normal again.

extraordinary ^{복습}
[ikstrɔ́:rdənèri]

a. 기이한, 놀라운; 비상한, 비범한
If you describe something as extraordinary, you mean that it is very unusual or surprising.

clap ^{복습}
[klæp]

v. 박수를 치다
When you clap, you hit your hands together to show appreciation or attract attention.

bargain**
[bá:rgən]

n. 거래, 매매 계약; 싼 물건, 특가품, 특매품
A bargain is an agreement, especially a formal business agreement, in which two people or groups agree what each of them will do, pay, or receive.

restore**
[ristɔ́r]

vt. 되돌리다, 복구하다, 회복시키다
To restore someone or something to a previous condition means to cause them to be in that condition once again.

perceive*
[pərsí:v]

vt. 지각하다, 감지하다
If you perceive something, you see, notice, or realize it, especially when it is not obvious.

glory*
[glɔ́:ri]

n. 영광; vi. 기뻐하다, 자랑으로 여기다
Glory is the fame and admiration that you gain by doing something impressive.

whisker ^{복습}
[wískər]

n. (고양이·쥐 등의) 수염; 구레나룻
The whiskers of an animal such as a cat or a mouse are the long stiff hairs that grow near its mouth.

repair[**] vt. 수리하다; n. 수리, 수선
[ripɛ́ər]
If you repair something that has been damaged or is not working properly, you mend it.

replace[보충] v. 대신하다, 대체하다
[ripléis]
If you replace something that is broken, damaged, or lost, you get a new one to use instead.

stun[*] vt. 어리벙벙하게 하다; 기절시키다; n. 놀라게 함 (stunning a. 굉장히 멋진)
[stʌn]
A stunning person or thing is extremely beautiful or impressive.

reap[*] v. 거두다, 획득하다; 베다, 수확하다
[ri:p]
If you reap the benefits or the rewards of something, you enjoy the good things that happen as a result of it.

investment[**] n. 투자; 투자액; 투자의 대상
[invɛ́stmənt]
Investment of time or effort is the spending of time or effort on something in order to make it a success.

1분에 몇 단어를 읽는지 리딩 속도를 측정해보세요.

$$\frac{346 \text{ words}}{\text{reading time (} \qquad \text{) sec}} \times 60 = (\qquad) \text{ WPM}$$

Build Your Vocabulary

mend**
[mend]

v. 고치다, 회복하다, 개선하다; n. 수선, 개량
If you mend something that is broken or not working, you repair it, so that it works properly or can be used.

polish**
[páliʃ]

v. 닦다, 윤내다; n. 광택; 세련 (polished a. 광이 나는)
If you polish something, you rub it with a cloth to make it shine.

elegant*복습
[éligənt]

a. 품위 있는, 우아한, 고상한
If you describe a person or thing as elegant, you mean that they are pleasing and graceful in appearance or style.

display*복습
[displéi]

n. 전시, 진열품; 표시; v. 보이다, 나타내다, 진열[전시]하다
A display is an arrangement of things that have been put in a particular place, so that people can see them easily.

workbench
[wɔ́:rkbèntʃ]

n. 작업대, 세공대
A workbench is a heavy wooden table on which people use tools such as a hammer and nails to make or repair things.

threshold**
[θréʃhould]

n. 문간, 문지방; 발단, 시초
The threshold of a building or room is the floor in the doorway, or the doorway itself.

flash*복습
[flæʃ]

v. 번쩍이다, 빛나다; n. 섬광, 번쩍임
If a light flashes or if you flash a light, it shines with a sudden bright light, especially as quick, regular flashes of light.

brilliant*복습
[bríljənt]

a. 빛나는, 찬란한, 훌륭한, 멋진 (brilliantly ad. 반짝반짝 (빛나게))
A brilliant color is extremely bright.

flood*복습
[flʌd]

v. 쇄도하다, 물밀듯이 밀려들다; 넘치다, 범람하다; n. 홍수; 쇄도, 폭주
If you say that a flood of people or things arrive somewhere, you are emphasizing that a very large number of them arrive there.

deal*복습
[di:l]

n. 거래; 대우; v. 거래하다; 다루다, 처리하다; 대우하다; 상대하다
If you make a deal, do a deal, or cut a deal, you complete an agreement or an arrangement with someone, especially in business.

sigh*복습
[sai]

v. 한숨 쉬다; n. 한숨, 탄식
When you sigh, you let out a deep breath, as a way of expressing feelings such as disappointment, tiredness, or pleasure.

moon***
[mu:n]

① v. (~을) 생각하면서 시간을 보내다, 서성거리다 ② n. 달
If you moon over something, you spend your time in a dream thinking about it that you love.

110

bust
[bʌst]

v. 부수다, 부서지다; (현장을) 덮치다; 파산하다
If you bust something, you break it or damage it so badly that it cannot be used.

repair^{복습}
[ripéər]

vt. 수리하다; n. 수리, 수선
If you repair something that has been damaged or is not working properly, you mend it.

bear^{복습}
[bɛər]

① v. 견디다; (의무·책임을) 지다; 낳다 ② n. 곰
If you bear an unpleasant experience, you accept it because you are unable to do anything about it.

mender^{복습}
[méndər]

n. 고치는 사람, 수선자
A mender is one who repairs something broken or not working.

tinkle
[tiŋkl]

v. 딸랑딸랑 울리다; n. 딸랑딸랑 하는 소리
If a bell tinkles or if you tinkle it, it makes a quiet ringing noise as you shake it.

1. How did Edward feel about the dolls around him?
   A. He was glad to finally have company around him.
   B. He wished that one of them could be a rabbit.
   C. He found them annoying and self-centered.
   D. He admired their beauty and charm.

2. Which of the following was NOT something that the first doll next to Edward said about him?
   A. She told him that he was in the wrong place.
   B. She told him that nobody was going to buy him.
   C. She told him that it was a store for dolls and not rabbits.
   D. She told him that someone might buy him if he waited long enough.

3. How did Edward react when the doll asked if he wanted to be loved?
   A. He told her that he had been loved by different people.
   B. He became silent and felt sad for all the people he had left.
   C. He told her that he never wanted to be loved again.
   D. He told her that he hoped he would finally learn about love.

4. How were Edward's expectations in the shop different from those of the dolls?
   A. The other dolls all expected to be loved, but Edward only expected to be hated.
   B. The other dolls all expected to be bought, but Edward didn't hope for anything.
   C. The other dolls all expected to be bought by children, but Edward liked Lucius Clarke taking care of him.
   D. The other dolls all expected to be forgotten, but Edward expected to be remembered forever.

5. Which of the following did NOT describe the new shelf mate for Edward?
   A. She was at least one hundred years old.
   B. Her head had been broken and repaired again.
   C. She was wearing a baby bonnet.
   D. She didn't talk to Edward at all.

6. How did the old doll remind Edward of Pellegrina?
   A. She mentioned a story about a princess and warthog.
   B. She and Pellegrina were both old.
   C. She said that Edward disappointed her.
   D. She had the same voice as Pellegrina.

7. How did Edward's attitude change after the old doll left?
   A. He became sad that she left so soon.
   B. He opened his heart and believed that someone would come for him.
   C. He decided that he would never open his heart to anyone again.
   D. He decided to completely forget about all his previous owners.

1분에 몇 단어를 읽는지 리딩 속도를 측정해보세요.

$$\frac{549 \text{ words}}{\text{reading time (} \quad \text{) sec}} \times 60 = (\qquad) \text{ WPM}$$

Build Your Vocabulary

technically
[téknikəli]
ad. 엄밀히 말해서; 전문적으로, 기술적으로
Technically means according to an exact understanding of rules or facts.

sailor
[séilər]
n. 뱃사람, 선원
A sailor is someone who works on a ship or sails a boat.

annoy^{복습}
[ənɔ́i]
v. 성가시게 굴다, 괴롭히다; 불쾌하다 (annoying a. 짜증나는, 남을 괴롭히는)
If someone or something annoys you, it makes you fairly angry and impatient.

self-centered
[sèlf-séntərd]
a. 자기 중심의, 이기적인
Someone who is self-centered is only concerned with their own wants and needs and never thinks about other people.

twitter^{복습}
[twítər]
v. 지저귀다, 지저귀듯 지껄이다; n. (새의) 지저귐; 흥분 (twittery a. 잘 지저귀는)
If you say that someone is twittering about something, you mean that they are speaking about silly or unimportant things, usually rather fast or in a high-pitched voice.

vain
[vein]
a. 자만심이 강한, 허영적인; 헛된, 무익한
If you describe someone as vain, you are critical of their extreme pride in their own beauty, intelligence, or other good qualities.

immediately^{복습}
[imí:diətli]
ad. 곧바로, 즉시
If something happens immediately, it happens without any delay.

reinforce
[ri:infɔ́:rs]
vt. 강화하다, 보강하다; 보충하다
If something reinforces a feeling, situation, or process, it makes that stronger or more intense.

high-pitched
[hái-pítʃt]
a. 음이 높고 날카로운
A high-pitched sound is shrill and high in pitch.

squeak
[skwi:k]
n. 찍찍 우는 소리; 삐걱거리는 소리; v. 끽끽거리며 말하다; (쥐 따위가) 찍찍 울다
If something or someone squeaks, they make a short, high-pitched sound.

shoo
[ʃu:]
int. 쉬이(개새 등을 쫓는 소리); v. 쉬이하고 소리를 쳐서 쫓다
You say 'shoo!' to an animal when you want it to go away.

obvious
[ábviəs]
a. 명백한, 분명한
If something is obvious, it is easy to see or understand.

114

elegant^{복습}
[éligənt]

a. 품위 있는, 우아한, 고상한
If you describe a person or thing as elegant, you mean that they are pleasing and graceful in appearance or style.

purchase^{**}
[pə́:rtʃəs]

vt. 사다, 구입하다; n. 구입, 매입, 획득
When you purchase something, you buy it.

gasp[*]
[gæsp]

v. (놀람 따위로) 숨이 막히다, 헐떡거리다; n. 헐떡거림
When you gasp, you take a short quick breath through your mouth, especially when you are surprised, shocked, or in pain.

note^{***}
[nout]

n. 음조, 음색; 메모, 기록; vt. 적다, 메모하다; 주의하다, 주목하다
In music, a note is the sound of a particular pitch, or a written symbol representing this sound.

hobo^{복습}
[hóubou]

n. 부랑자, 떠돌이
A hobo is a person who has no home, especially one who travels from place to place and gets money by begging.

impassioned
[impǽʃənd]

a. 열정적인, 간절한
An impassioned speech or piece of writing is one in which someone expresses their strong feelings about an issue in a forceful way.

considerable^{복습}
[kənsídərəbl]

a. 상당한, 꽤 많은; 다수[다량]의; 중요한
Considerable means great in amount or degree.

pluck^{**}
[plʌk]

v. 골라내다, 뽑다, 잡아 뜯다; n. 잡아 뜯기; 담력, 용기
If you pluck something from somewhere, you take it between your fingers and pull it sharply from where it is.

good riddance

idiom 보기 싫은 것이 없어서 속이 시원하다
You say 'good riddance' to indicate that you are pleased that someone has left or that something has gone.

spot^{복습}
[spat]

n. 장소, 지점; 반점, 얼룩; vt. 발견하다, 분별하다
You can refer to a particular place as a spot.

vacant^{**}
[véikənt]

a. 빈, 비어 있는; 공허한
If something is vacant, it is not being used by anyone.

swing^{복습}
[swiŋ]

v. (swung–swung) (한 점을 축으로 하여) 빙 돌다, 휙 움직이다; 휘두르다
If something swings in a particular direction or if you swing it in that direction, it moves in that direction with a smooth, curving movement.

contrarian
[kəntréəriən]

n. 반대 의견을 가진 사람; a. 반대 의견의
A contrarian is a person who deliberately behaves in a way that is different from the people around them.

pride^{**}
[praid]

vt. 자랑하다; n. 자존심, 긍지; 만족감
If you pride yourself on a quality or skill that you have, you are very proud of it.

immobile
[imóubi:l]

a. 움직이지 않는, 불변의
Someone or something that is immobile is completely still.

dusk^{복습}
[dʌsk]

n. 땅거미, 황혼, 어스름
Dusk is the time just before night when the daylight has almost gone but when it is not completely dark.

1분에 몇 단어를 읽는지 리딩 속도를 측정해보세요.

$$\frac{836 \text{ words}}{\text{reading time } (\quad) \text{ sec}} \times 60 = (\quad) \text{ WPM}$$

Build Your Vocabulary

mender ^{복습}
[méndər]

n. 고치는 사람, 수선자
A mender is one who repairs something broken or not working.

gloom ^{**}
[glu:m]

n. 어둠침침함, 어둠, 그늘
The gloom is a state of near darkness.

repair ^{복습}
[ripéər]

vt. 수리하다; n. 수리, 수선
If you repair something that has been damaged or is not working properly, you mend it.

crack ^{복습}
[kræk]

n. 갈라진 금; 갑작스런 날카로운 소리;
v. 금이 가다, 깨(지)다; 날카로운 소리를 내다
A crack is a very narrow gap between two things, or between two parts of a thing.

bonnet [*]
[bánit]

n. 보닛(턱 밑에서 끈을 매는 어린이용의 챙 없는 모자)
A bonnet is a hat with ribbons that are tied under the chin. Bonnets are now worn by babies.

acquaintance ^{**}
[əkwéintəns]

n. 아는 사람, 지인
An acquaintance is someone who you have met and know slightly, but not well.

heavenly ^{**}
[hévənli]

a. 훌륭한, 천국 같은; 하늘의, 창공의
Something that is heavenly is very pleasant and enjoyable.

horrid [*]
[hɔ́:rid]

a. 무시무시한; 매우 불쾌한, 지겨운
If you describe something as horrid, you mean that it is very unpleasant indeed.

confirm ^{**}
[kənfə́:rm]

vt. 입증하다, 확인하다, 굳게 하다
If you confirm something that has been stated or suggested, you say that it is true because you know about it.

mend ^{복습}
[mend]

v. 고치다, 회복하다, 개선하다; n. 수선, 개량
If you mend something that is broken or not working, you repair it, so that it works properly or can be used.

adventure ^{**}
[ædvéntʃər]

n. 모험, 뜻하지 않은 경험; v. 위험을 무릅쓰다
If someone has an adventure, they become involved in an unusual, exciting, and rather dangerous journey or series of events.

century ^{***}
[séntʃəri]

n. 1세기, 100년
A century is any period of a hundred years.

116

wonder^{복습}
[wʌ́ndər]

v. 이상하게 여기다, 호기심을 가지다; n. 경탄할 만한 것, 경이
If you wonder about something, you think about it because it interests you and you want to know more about it.

dreadful**
[drédfəl]

a. 끔찍한, 지독한; 무시무시한
If you say that something is dreadful, you mean that it is very bad or unpleasant, or very poor in quality.

expectancy
[ikspéktənsi]

n. 기대, 예상, 예기
Expectancy is the feeling or hope that something exciting, interesting, or good is about to happen.

awash
[əwɔ́ʃ]

a. (~으로) 가득 차, 넘쳐
If a place is awash with something, it contains a large amount of it.

courage***
[kə́:ridʒ]

n. 용기, 담력
Courage is the quality shown by someone who decides to do something difficult or dangerous, even though they may be afraid.

intention**
[inténʃən]

n. 의향, 의지, 목적, 의도
An intention is an idea or plan of what you are going to do.

journey***
[dʒə́:rni]

n. 여정, 여행
When you make a journey, you travel from one place to another.

pointless^{복습}
[pɔ́intlis]

a. 무의미한, 할 가치가 없는
If you say that something is pointless, you are criticizing it because it has no sense or purpose.

leap^{복습}
[li:p]

v. 껑충 뛰다; 뛰어넘다; n. 뜀, 도약
If you leap, you jump high in the air or jump a long distance.

shatter**
[ʃǽtər]

v. 산산조각이 나다; 파괴하다; n. 파편, 부서진 조각
If something shatters or is shattered, it breaks into a lot of small pieces.

get something over with

idiom (싫은 일 등을) 끝마치다, 완성하다
If you get something necessary but unpleasant over with, you bring it to an end.

mutter^{복습}
[mʌ́tər]

v. 중얼거리다, 불평하다; n. 중얼거림, 불평
If you mutter, you speak very quietly so that you cannot easily be heard, often because you are complaining about something.

stare^{복습}
[stɛər]

v. 응시하다, 뚫어지게 보다
If you stare at someone or something, you look at them for a long time.

spell**
[spel]

n. 주문(呪文), 주술; 마력, 마법; v. (낱말을) 맞춤법에 따라 쓰다, 철자를 말하다
A spell is a situation in which events are controlled by a magical power.

curse**
[kə:rs]

n. 저주, 악담; vt. 저주하다, 욕설을 퍼붓다
If you say that there is a curse on someone, you mean that there seems to be a supernatural power causing unpleasant things to happen to them.

stir[*]
[stəːr]

v. 움직이다; 휘젓다, 뒤섞다; n. 움직임; 휘젓기
If a particular memory, feeling, or mood stirs or is stirred in you, you begin to think about it or feel it.

shade^{**}
[ʃeid]

n. 블라인드(빛·열을 가리는 것); 색조; 그늘, 음영; vt. 그늘지게 하다
A shade is a piece of stiff cloth or heavy paper that you can pull down over a window as a covering.

switch^{**}
[switʃ]

v. 바꾸다, 교환하다; 스위치를 넣다[돌리다]; n. 스위치
If you switch two things, you replace one with the other.

nod^{복습}
[nad]

v. 끄덕이다, 끄덕여 표시하다; n. (동의·인사·신호·명령의) 끄덕임
If you nod, you move your head downward and upward to show agreement, understanding, or approval.

antique[*]
[æntíːk]

n. 골동품; a. 골동품의; 구식의
An antique is an old object such as a piece of china or furniture which is valuable because of its beauty or rarity.

firm^{복습}
[fəːrm]

① a. 굳은, 단단한; 견고한 (firmly ad. 굳게) ② n. 회사
If you describe someone as firm, you mean they behave in a way that shows that they are not going to change their mind, or that they are the person who is in control.

sigh^{복습}
[sai]

n. 한숨, 탄식 v. 한숨 쉬다
A sigh is a deep breath, as a way of expressing feelings such as disappointment, tiredness, or pleasure.

shaft[*]
[ʃæft]

n. 한 줄기의 광선; (보통 건물·지하의) 수직 통로
A shaft of light is a beam of light, for example sunlight shining through an opening.

flood^{복습}
[flʌd]

v. 쇄도하다, 물밀듯이 밀려들다; 넘치다, 범람하다; n. 홍수; 쇄도, 폭주
If light floods a place or floods into it, it suddenly fills it.

wind^{복습}
[waind]

① v. 감다, 돌리다; n. 한 번 돌리기, 한 번 감음 ② n. 바람
When you wind something flexible around something else, you wrap it around it several times.

bend^{**}
[bend]

v. 굽히다, 구부리다; (방향이) 구부러지다, 휘다
When you bend, you move the top part of your body downward and forward.

1. What phrase did Edward repeat to himself in the doll shop?

   A. Someone will come.

   B. It will be alright.

   C. Open your heart.

   D. Love is powerful.

2. How did the little girl react when she saw Edward?

   A. She smiled and stared at Edward without touching him.

   B. She frowned and walked past Edward.

   C. She took Edward off the shelf and cradled him.

   D. She laughed at the only rabbit in the doll shop.

3. What did Lucius Clarke tell the girl's mother when the girl handled Edward?

   A. He told her mother to watch her because Edward was fragile and expensive.

   B. He told her that Edward would be perfect for little girls.

   C. He told her that Edward was not for sale because he was an antique.

   D. He told her that another doll would be much better for her.

4. What was special about the locket around the woman's neck?

A. It had a photo of Edward inside it.

B. It was Edward's gold pocket watch.

C. It was made of solid silver.

D. It had her daughter's name written on it.

5. Who did Edward dance together with in the garden at the end of the story?

A. He danced with Pellegrina.

B. He danced with Abilene.

C. He danced with Abilene's daughter.

D. He danced with Abilene's son.

1분에 몇 단어를 읽는지 리딩 속도를 측정해보세요.

$$\frac{404 \text{ words}}{\text{reading time (\quad) sec}} \times 60 = (\quad) \text{ WPM}$$

Build Your Vocabulary

outrage
[áutreidʒ]

v. 격분시키다; (법률·도의 등을) 위반하다; n. 격분, 분개; 불법, 난폭
(outrageous a. 멋진, 근사한; 난폭한; 지나친)
If you are outraged by something, it makes you extremely shocked and angry.

collector[*]
[kəléktər]

n. 수집가; 수금원
A collector is a person who collects things of a particular type as a hobby.

wear^{***}
[wɛər]

v. (wore~worn) (구멍·홈을) 파다; 닳다, 낡다, 해지다; 입고 있다
If something wears, it becomes thinner or weaker because it is constantly being used over a long period of time.

smooth^{***}
[smu:ð]

a. 매끄러운; 유창한; v. 매끄럽게 하다[되다]
You use smooth to describe something that is going well and is free of problems or trouble.

groove[*]
[gru:v]

n. 홈, 파인 곳; 리듬(감); vt. 리듬을 타다
A groove is a deep line cut into a surface.

blossom^{**}
[blásəm]

n. 꽃; vi. 꽃 피다, 개화하다; 발전하다, 번영하다
Blossom is the flowers that appear on a tree before the fruit.

struggle^{**}
[strʌgl]

v. 분투하다, 고심하다; 발버둥 치다, 몸부림치다; n. 발버둥질, 노력
If you struggle to do something, you try hard to do it, even though other people or things may be making it difficult for you to succeed.

stare
[stɛər]

v. 응시하다, 똑바로 보다
If you stare at someone or something, you look at them for a long time.

solemn[*]
[sáləm]

a. 엄숙한, 근엄한 (solemnly ad. 장엄하게, 엄숙하게)
Someone or something that is solemn is very serious rather than cheerful or humorous.

cradle
[kreidl]

v. (안전하게 보호하듯이) 떠받치다, 살짝 안다; n. 유아용 침대; (전화의) 수화기대
If you cradle someone or something in your arms or hands, you hold them carefully and gently.

ferocious
[fəróuʃəs]

a. 대단한, 맹렬한; 잔인한, 지독한, 사나운
If you describe actions or feelings as ferocious, you mean that they are intense and determined.

tender*
[téndər]

a. 부드러운, 상냥한, 다정한
Someone or something that is tender expresses gentle and caring feelings.

attend***
[əténd]

v. ~에 주의를 기울이다; 출석하다
If you attend to something, you deal with it.

fragile*
[frǽdʒəl]

a. 부서지기[깨지기] 쉬운
Something that is fragile is easily broken or damaged.

precious*
[préʃəs]

a. 귀중한, 가치가 있는, 비싼
Precious objects and materials are worth a lot of money because they are rare.

dizzy*
[dízi]

a. 현기증 나는, 아찔한
If you feel dizzy, you feel as if everything is spinning round and being unable to balance.

wonder복습
[wʌ́ndəːr]

v. 이상하게 여기다, 호기심을 가지다; n. 경탄할 만한 것, 경이
If you wonder about something, you think about it because it interests you and you want to know more about it.

crack복습
[kræk]

v. 깨(지)다, 금이 가다; 날카로운 소리를 내다; n. 갈라진 금; 갑작스런 날카로운 소리
If something hard cracks, or if you crack it, it becomes slightly damaged, with lines appearing on its surface.

hang복습
[hæŋ]

v. (hung–hung) 걸다, 달아매다; 매달리다, 달려 있다; 배회하다; 교수형에 처하다
If something hangs in a high place or position, or if you hang it there, it is attached there so it does not touch the ground.

Check Your Reading Speed

1분에 몇 단어를 읽는지 리딩 속도를 측정해보세요.

$$\frac{188 \text{ words}}{\text{reading time ( ) sec}} \times 60 = (\qquad) \text{ WPM}$$

Build Your Vocabulary

journey ^{복습}
[dʒə́ːrni]

n. 여정, 여행
When you make a journey, you travel from one place to another.

overboard ^{복습}
[óuvərbɔ̀ːrd]

ad. 배 밖으로[에]
If you fall overboard, you fall over the side of a boat into the water.

rescue ^{복습}
[réskjuː]

vt. 구조하다, 구출하다; n. 구출, 구원
If you rescue someone, you get them out of a dangerous or unpleasant situation.

bury ^{복습}
[béri]

vt. 묻다, 파묻다, 매장하다
To bury something means to put it into a hole in the ground and cover it up with earth.

garbage ^{복습}
[gɑ́rbidʒ]

n. 쓰레기, 찌꺼기
Garbage consists of unwanted things or waste material such as used paper, empty tins and bottles, and waste food.

hobo ^{복습}
[hóubou]

n. 부랑자, 떠돌이
A hobo is a person who has no home, especially one who travels from place to place and gets money by begging.

scarecrow ^{복습}
[skéərkròu]

n. 허수아비
A scarecrow is an object in the shape of a person, which is put in a field where crops are growing in order to frighten birds away.

diner ^{복습}
[dáinər]

n. 간이 식당; 식사하는 사람
A diner is a small cheap restaurant that is open all day.

mender ^{복습}
[méndər]

n. 고치는 사람, 수선자
A mender is one who repairs something broken or not working.

swear ^{**}
[swɛər]

v. (swore—sworn) 맹세하다, 단언하다; n. 맹세, 선서
If you swear to do something, you promise in a serious way that you will do it.

swing ^{복습}
[swiŋ]

v. (swung—swung) (한 점을 축으로 하여) 빙 돌다, 휙 움직이다; 휘두르다
If something swings in a particular direction or if you swing it in that direction, it moves in that direction with a smooth, curving movement.

marvelous ^{**}
[mɑ́ːrvələs]

a. 놀라운, 믿기 어려운; 훌륭한, 우수한
If you describe someone or something as marvelous, you are emphasizing that they are very good.

수고하셨습니다!

드디어 끝까지 다 읽으셨군요! 축하드립니다! 여러분은 이 책을 통해 총 17,050개의 단어를 읽으셨고, 700개 이상의 어휘와 표현들을 익히셨습니다. 이 책에 나온 어휘는 다른 원서를 읽을 때에도 빈번히 만날 수 있는 필수 어휘들입니다. 이 책을 읽었던 경험은 비슷한 수준의 다른 원서들을 읽을 때 큰 도움이 될 것입니다.

이제 자신의 상황에 맞게 원서를 반복해서 읽거나, 오디오북을 들어 볼 수 있습니다. 혹은 비슷한 수준의 다른 원서를 찾아 읽는 것도 좋습니다. 일단 원서를 완독한 뒤에 어떻게 계속 영어 공부를 이어갈 수 있을지, 도움말을 꼼꼼히 살펴보고 각자 상황에 맞게 적용해 보세요!

리딩(Reading)을 확실하게 다지고 싶다면? 반복해서 읽어 보세요!

리딩 실력을 탄탄하게 다지고 싶다면, 같은 원서를 2~3번 반복해서 읽을 것을 권합니다. 같은 책을 여러 번 읽으면 지루할 것 같지만, 꼭 그렇지도 않습니다. 반복해서 읽을 때 처음과 주안점을 다르게 두면, 전혀 다른 느낌으로 재미있게 읽을 수 있습니다.

처음 원서를 읽을 때는 생소한 단어들과 스토리로 인해 읽으면서 곧바로 이해하기가 매우 힘들 수 있습니다. 전체 맥락을 잡고 읽어도 약간 버거운 느낌이지요. 하지만 반복해서 읽기 시작하면 달라집니다. 일단 내용을 파악한 상황이기 때문에 문장 구조나 어휘의 활용에 더 집중하게 되고, 조금 더 깊이 있게 읽을 수 있습니다. 좋은 표현과 문장을 수집하고 메모할 만한 여유도 생기게 되지요. 어휘도 많이 익숙해졌기 때문에 리딩 속도에도 탄력이 붙습니다. 처음 읽을 때는 '내용'에서 재미를 느꼈다면, 반복해서 읽을 때에는 '영어'에서 재미를 느끼게 되는 것입니다. 따라서 리딩 실력을 더욱 확고하게 다지고자 한다면, 같은 책을 2~3회 정도 반복해서 읽을 것을 권해 드립니다.

리스닝(Listening) 실력을 늘리고 싶다면?
귀를 통해서 읽어 보세요!

많은 영어 학습자들이 '리스닝이 안 돼서 문제'라고 한탄합니다. 그리고 리스닝 실력을 늘리는 방법으로 무슨 뜻인지 몰라도 반복해서 듣는 '무작정 듣기'를 선택합니다. 하지만 뜻도 모르면서 무작정 듣는 일에는 엄청난 인내력이 필요합니다. 그래서 대부분 며칠 시도하다가 포기해 버리고 말지요.

따라서 모르는 내용을 무작정 듣는 것보다는 어느 정도 알고 있는 내용을 반복해서 듣는 것이 더 효과적인 듣기 방법입니다. 그리고 이런 방식의 듣기에 활용할 수 있는 가장 좋은 교재가 오디오북입니다.

리스닝 실력을 향상하고 싶다면, 이 책에서 제공하는 오디오북을 이용해서 듣는 연습을 해 보세요. 활용법은 간단합니다. 일단 책을 한 번 완독했다면, 오디오북을 통해 다시 들어 보는 것입니다. 휴대 기기에 넣어 시간이 날 때 틈틈이 듣는 것도 좋고, 책상에 앉아 눈으로는 텍스트를 보며 귀로 읽는 것도 좋습니다. 이미 읽었던 내용이라 이해하기가 훨씬 수월하고, 애매했던 발음들도 자연스럽게 교정할 수 있습니다. 또 성우의 목소리 연기를 듣다 보면 내용이 더욱 생동감 있게 다가와 이해도가 높아지는 효과도 거둘 수 있습니다.

반대로 듣기에 자신 있는 사람이라면, 책을 읽기 전에 처음부터 오디오북을 먼저 듣는 것도 좋은 방법입니다. 귀를 통해 책을 쭉 읽어보고, 이후에 다시 눈으로 책을 읽으면서 잘 들리지 않았던 부분들을 보충하는 것이지요.

중요한 것은 내용을 따라가면서, 내용에 푹 빠져서 반복해 들어야 한다는 것입니다. 이렇게 연습을 반복해서 눈으로 읽지 않은 책이라도 '귀를 통해' 읽을 수 있을 정도가 되면, 리스닝으로 고생하는 일은 거의 없을 것입니다.

왼쪽의 QR 코드를 스마트폰으로 인식하여 정식 오디오북을 들어 보세요! 더불어 롱테일북스 홈페이지(www.longtailbooks.co.kr)에서도 오디오북 MP3 파일을 다운로드 받을 수 있습니다.

스피킹(Speaking)이 고민이라면? 소리 내어 읽어 보세요!

스피킹 역시 많은 학습자들이 고민하는 부분입니다. 스피킹이 고민이라면, 원서를 큰 소리로 읽는 낭독 훈련(Voice Reading)을 해 보세요!

'소리 내어 읽는 것이 말하기에 정말로 도움이 될까?'라고 의아한 생각이 들 수도 있습니다. 하지만 인간의 두뇌 입장에서 봤을 때, 성대 구조를 활용해서 '발화'한다는 점에서는 소리 내어 읽기와 말하기에 큰 차이가 없다고 합니다. 소리 내어 읽는 것은 '타인의 생각'을 전달하고, 직접 말하는 것은 '자신의 생각'을 전달한다는 차이가 있을 뿐, 머릿속에서 문장을 처리하고 조음기관(혀와 성대 등)을 움직여 의미를 만든다는 점에서 같은 과정인 것이지요. 따라서 소리 내어 읽는 연습을 꾸준히 하는 것은 스피킹 연습에 큰 도움이 됩니다.

소리 내어 읽기를 하는 방법은 간단합니다. 일단 오디오북을 들으면서 성우의 목소리를 최대한 따라 하며 같이 읽어 보세요. 발음뿐 아니라 억양, 어조, 느낌까지 완벽히 따라 한다고 생각하면서 소리 내어 읽습니다. 따라 읽는 것이 조금 익숙해지면, 옆의 누군가에게 이 책을 읽어 준다는 생각으로 소리 내어 계속 읽어 나갑니다. 한 번 눈과 귀로 읽었던 책이기 때문에 보다 수월하게 진행할 수 있고, 자연스럽게 어휘와 표현을 복습하는 효과도 거두게 됩니다. 또 이렇게 소리 내어 읽은 것을 녹음해서 들어 보면 스스로에게도 좋은 피드백이 됩니다.

최근 말하기가 강조되면서 소리 내어 읽기가 크게 각광을 받고 있기는 하지만, 그렇다고 소리 내어 읽기가 무조건 좋은 것만은 아닙니다. 책을 소리 내어 읽다 보면, 무의식적으로 속으로 발음을 하는 습관을 가지게 되어 리딩 속도 자체는 오히려 크게 떨어지는 현상이 발생할 수 있습니다. 따라서 빠른 리딩 속도가 중요한 수험생이나 상위권 학습자들에게는 소리 내어 읽기가 적절하지 않은 방법입니다. 효과가 좋다는 말만 믿고 무턱대고 따라 하기보다는 자신의 필요에 맞게 우선순위를 정하고 원서를 활용하는 것이 좋습니다.

라이팅(Writing)까지 욕심이 난다면? 요약하는 연습을 해 보세요!

원서를 라이팅 연습에 직접적으로 활용하는 데에는 한계가 있지만, 적절히 활용하면 원서도 유용한 라이팅 자료가 될 수 있습니다.

특히 책을 읽고 그 내용을 요약하는 연습은 큰 도움이 됩니다. 요약 훈련의 방식도 간단합니다. 원서를 읽고 그날 읽은 분량만큼 혹은 책을 다 읽고 전체 내용을 기반으로, 책 내용을 한번 요약하고 나의 느낌을 영어로 적어보는 것입니다.

이때 그 책에 나왔던 단어와 표현을 최대한 활용하여 요약하는 것이 중요합니다. 영어 표현력은 결국 얼마나 다양한 어휘로 많은 표현을 해 보았느냐가 좌우하게 됩니다. 이런 면에서 내가 읽은 책을, 그 책에 나온 문장과 어휘로 다시 표현해 보는 것은 매우 효율적인 방법입니다. 책에 나온 어휘와 표현을 단순히 읽고 무슨 말인지 아는 정도가 아니라, 실제로 직접 활용해서 쓸 수 있을 만큼 확실하게 익히게 되는 것이지요. 여기에 첨삭까지 받을 수 있는 방법이 있다면 금상첨화입니다.

이러한 '표현하기' 연습은 스피킹 훈련에도 그대로 적용될 수 있습니다. 책을 읽고 그 내용을 3분 안에 다른 사람에게 영어로 말하는 연습을 해 보세요. 순발력과 표현력을 기르는 좋은 훈련이 될 것입니다.

꾸준히 원서를 읽고 싶다면? 뉴베리 수상작을 계속 읽어 보세요!

뉴베리 상이 세계 최고 권위의 아동 문학상인 만큼, 그 수상작들은 확실히 완성도를 검증받은 작품이라고 할 수 있습니다. 특히 '쉬운 어휘로 쓰인 깊이 있는 문장'으로 이루어졌다는 점이 영어 학습자들에게 큰 호응을 얻고 있습니다. 이렇게 '검증된 원서'를 꾸준히 읽는 것은 영어 실력 향상에 큰 도움이 됩니다.

아래에 수준별로 제시된 뉴베리 수상작 목록을 보며 적절한 책들을 찾아 계속 읽어 보세요. 꼭 뉴베리 수상작이 아니더라도 마음에 드는 작가의 다른 책을 읽어 보는 것 또한 아주 좋은 방법입니다.

• 영어 초보자도 쉽게 읽을 만한 아주 쉬운 수준. 소리 내어 읽기에도 아주 적합.
Sarah, Plain and Tall*(Medal, 8,331단어), The Hundred Penny Box (Honor, 5,878단어), The Hundred Dresses*(Honor, 7,329단어), My Father's Dragon (Honor, 7,682단어), 26 Fairmount Avenue (Honor, 6,737단어)

• 중·고등학생 정도 영어 학습자라면 쉽게 읽을 수 있는 수준. 소리 내어 읽기에도 비교적 적합한 편.

Because of Winn-Dixie*(Honor, 22,123단어), What Jamie Saw (Honor, 17,203단어), Charlotte's Web (Honor, 31,938단어), Dear Mr. Henshaw (Medal, 18,145단어), Missing May (Medal, 17,509단어)

• 대학생 정도 영어 학습자라면 무난한 수준. 소리 내어 읽기에 적합하지 않음.

Number The Stars*(Medal, 27,197단어), A Single Shard (Medal, 33,726단어), The Tale of Despereaux*(Medal, 32,375단어), Hatchet*(Medal, 42,328단어), Bridge to Terabithia (Medal, 32,888단어), A Fine White Dust (Honor, 19,022단어), Jennifer, Hecate, Macbeth, William McKinley and Me, Elizabeth (Honor, 23,266단어)

• 원서 완독 경험을 가진 학습자에게 적절한 수준. 소리 내어 읽기에 적합하지 않음.

The Giver*(Medal, 43,617단어), From the Mixed-Up Files of Mrs. Basil E. Frankweiler (Medal, 30,906단어), The View from Saturday (Medal, 42,685단어), Holes*(Medal, 47,079단어), Criss Cross (Medal, 48,221단어), Walk Two Moons (Medal, 59,400단어), The Graveyard Book (Medal, 67,380단어)

뉴베리 수상작과 뉴베리 수상 작가의 좋은 작품을 엄선한 「뉴베리 컬렉션」에도 위 목록에 있는 도서 중 상당수가 포함될 예정입니다.

★ 「뉴베리 컬렉션」으로 이미 출간된 도서

어떤 책들이 출간되었는지 확인하려면, 지금 인터넷서점에서 ▒▒▒▒▒▒▒을 검색해보세요.

뉴베리 수상작을 동영상 강의로 만나 보세요!

영어원서 전문 동영상 강의 사이트 영서당(yseodang.com)에서는 뉴베리 컬렉션 『Holes』, 『Because of Winn-Dixie』, 『The Miraculous Journey of Edward Tulane』, 『Wayside School』 시리즈 등의 동영상 강의를 제공하고 있습니다. 뉴베리 수상작이라는 최고의 영어 교재와 EBS 출신 인기 강사가 만난 명강의! 지금 사이트를 방문해서 무료 샘플 강의를 들어 보세요!

'스피드 리딩 카페'를 통해 원서 읽기 습관을 길러 보세요!

일상에서 영어를 한마디도 쓰지 않는 비영어권 국가에서 살고 있는 우리가 영어 환경에 가장 쉽고, 편하고, 부담 없이 노출되는 방법은 바로 '영어원서 읽기'입니다. 언제 어디서든 원서를 붙잡고 읽기만 하면 곧바로 영어를 접하는 환경이 만들어지기 때문이지요. 하루에 20분씩만 꾸준히 읽는다면, 1년에 무려 120시간 동안 영어에 노출될 수 있습니다. 이러한 이유 때문에 영어 교육 전문가들이 영어 원서 읽기를 추천하는 것이지요.

하지만 원서 읽기가 좋다는 것을 알아도 막상 꾸준히 읽는 것은 쉽지 않습니다. 그럴 때에는 13만 명 이상의 회원을 보유한 국내 최대 원서 읽기 동호회 〈스피드 리딩 카페〉(cafe.naver.com/readingtc)를 방문해 보세요.

원서별로 정리된 무료 PDF 단어장과 수준별 추천 원서 목록 등 유용한 자료는 물론, 뉴베리 수상작을 포함한 다양한 원서의 리뷰를 무료로 확인할 수 있습니다. 특히 함께 모여서 원서를 읽는 '북클럽'은 중간에 포기하지 않고 원서를 끝까지 읽는 습관을 기르는 데 큰 도움이 될 것입니다.

Chapters One & Two

1. C   Once, in a house on Egypt Street, there lived a rabbit who was made almost entirely of china. He had china arms and china legs, china paws and a china head, a china torso and a china nose.

2. D   Of all the seasons of the year, the rabbit most preferred winter, for the sun set early then and the dining room windows became dark and Edward could see his own reflection in the glass.

3. B   Once, in a house on Egypt Street, there lived a rabbit who was made almost entirely of china. . . . Edward's mistress was a ten-year-old, dark-haired girl named Abilene Tulane, who thought almost as highly of Edward as Edward thought of himself.

4. A   It was Pellegrina who was responsible for Edward's existence. It was she who had commissioned his making, she who had ordered his silk suits and his pocket watch, his jaunty hats and his bendable ears, his fine leather shoes and his jointed arms and legs, all from a master craftsman in her native France. It was Pellegrina who had given him as a gift to Abilene on her seventh birthday.

5. D   Abilene balanced the watch on his left leg. She kissed the tips of his ears, and then she left and Edward spent the day staring out at Egypt Street, listening to the tick of his watch and waiting.

6. C   Edward's silk suit was stained with drool and his head ached for several days afterward, but it was his ego that had suffered the most damage.

7. A   The rabbit, too, was experiencing a great emotion. But it was not love. It was annoyance that he had been so mightily inconvenienced, that he had been handled by the maid as cavalierly as an inanimate object – a serving bowl, say, or a teapot.

1. A   Edward, of course, was not listening. He found the talk around the dinner table excruciatingly dull; in fact, he made a point of not listening if he could help it.

2. B   She was looking at him in the way a hawk hanging lazily in the air might study a mouse on the ground. Perhaps the rabbit fur on Edward's ears and tail, and the whiskers on his nose had some dim memory of being hunted, for a shiver went through him.

3. C   "Why did it make no difference?" asked Abilene. "Because," said Pellegrina, "she was a princess who loved no one and cared nothing for love, even though there were many who loved her."

4. C   "She swallowed the ring. She took it from her finger and swallowed it. She said, 'That is what I think of love.' And she ran from the prince. She left the castle and went deep into the woods. And so."

5. D   " 'I love no one,' said the princess proudly. 'You disappoint me,' said the witch. She raised her hand and said one word: 'Farthfigery.' And the beautiful princess was changed into a warthog. . . ."

6. A   She leaned close to him. She whispered, "You disappoint me."

7. B   The story, he thought, had been pointless. But then most stories were.

Chapters Five & Six

1. C   The house on Egypt Street became frantic with activity as the Tulane family prepared for their voyage to England.

2. B   As was to be expected, Edward Tulane exacted much attention on board the ship.

3. C   "What does he do?" Martin asked Abilene on their second day at sea. He pointed at Edward, who was sitting on a deckchair with his long legs stretched in front of him. . . . It came as a total surprise to him when he was grabbed off the deckchair and first his scarf, and then his jacket and trousers, were ripped from his body. . . . Martin threw Edward. And Edward sailed naked through the air.

4. A   Only a moment ago, the rabbit had thought that being naked in front of a shipload of strangers was the worst thing that could happen to him. But he was wrong. It was much worse being tossed, in the same naked state, from the hands of one grubby, laughing boy to another.

5. C   Amos raised his arm, but just as he was getting ready to throw Edward, Abilene tackled him, shoving her head into his stomach, and upsetting the boy's aim. So it was that Edward did not go flying back into the dirty hands of Martin. Instead, Edward Tulane went overboard.

6. B   My pocket watch, he thought. I need that.

7. D   The china rabbit landed, finally, on the ocean floor, face down; and there, with his head in the muck, he experienced his first genuine and true emotion. Edward Tulane was afraid.

Chapters Seven & Eight

1. A   He told himself that certainly Abilene would come and find him. This, Edward thought, is much like waiting for Abilene to come home from school.

2. D   And then the rabbit thought about Pellegrina. He felt, in some way that he could not explain to himself, that she was responsible for what had happened to him. It was almost as if it was she, and not the boys, who had thrown Edward overboard.

3. B   The storm was so powerful that it lifted Edward off the ocean floor and led him in a crazy, wild and spinning dance. The water pummeled him and lifted him up and shoved him back down.

4. C   "I'll take it home to Nellie. Let her fix it up and set it to rights. Give it to some child."

5. B   On land, the old fisherman stopped to light a pipe, and then, with the pipe clenched between his teeth, he walked home, carrying Edward atop his left shoulder as if he were a conquering hero.

6. A   "There you are, now," said the fisherman. He took the pipe out of his mouth and pointed with the stem of it at a star in the purpling sky. "There's your North Star right there. Don't never have to be lost when you know where that fellow is."

7. D   "She's beautiful," breathed Nellie. For a moment, Edward was confused. Was there some other object of beauty in the room? "What will I call her?" "Susanna?" said Lawrence.

Chapters Nine & Ten

1. D   Nellie loved to bake, and so she spent her day in the kitchen. She put Edward

on the counter and leaned him up against the flour canister and arranged his dress around his knees.

2. A   And Edward was surprised to discover that he was listening. Before, when Abilene talked to him, everything had seemed so boring, so pointless. But now, the stories Nellie told struck him as the most important thing in the world and he listened as if his life depended on what she said.

3. C   In the evening, Lawrence came home from the sea and there was dinner and Edward sat at the table with the fisherman and his wife. He sat in an old wooden high chair; and while at first he was mortified (a high chair, after all, was a chair designed for babies, not for elegant rabbits), he soon became used to it.

4. A   Every night after dinner, Lawrence said that he thought he would go out and get some fresh air and that maybe Susanna would like to come with him. He placed Edward on his shoulder as he had that first night when he walked him through town, bringing him home to Nellie.

5. A   "What's this?" she said. She put down her suitcase and picked Edward up by one foot. She held him upside down. "That's Susanna," said Nellie. "Susanna!" shouted Lolly. She gave Edward a shake. His dress was up over his head and he could see nothing. Already, he had formed a deep and abiding hatred for Lolly.

6. C   Of course, after dinner Edward did not go outside and stand beneath the stars to have a smoke with Lawrence. And Nellie, for the first time since Edward had been with her, did not sing him a lullaby. In fact, Edward was ignored and forgotten about until the next morning, when Lolly picked him up again and pulled his dress down away from his face and stared him in the eye.

7. B   Edward felt a sharp pain somewhere deep inside his china chest. For the first time, his heart called out to him. It said two words: Nellie. Lawrence.

Chapters Eleven & Twelve

1. D   The first night, he was at the top of the rubbish heap, and so he was able to look up at the stars and find comfort in their light.

2. B   In the morning, a short man came climbing through the rubbish. He stopped when he was standing on top of the highest pile. He put his hands under his armpits and flapped his elbows. The man crowed loudly. He shouted, "Who am I? I'm Ernest, Ernest who is king of the world."

3. C   Day after day passed, and Edward was aware of time passing only because every

morning he could hear Ernest performing his dawn ritual, cackling and crowing about being king of the world.

4. B   The rubbish around him shifted, and the rabbit heard the sniffing and panting of a dog. Then came the frenzied sound of digging. The rubbish shifted again, and suddenly, miraculously, the beautiful, buttery light of late afternoon shone on Edward's face.

5. C   The sun was shining and Edward felt exhilarated. Who, having known him before, would have thought that he could be so happy now, crusted over with rubbish, wearing a dress, held in the slobbery mouth of a dog and being chased by a madman? But he was happy.

6. A   He gave Edward a playful shake. "You're some child's toy, am I right? And you have been separated, somehow, from the child who loves you." Edward felt, again, the sharp pain in his chest. He thought of Abilene. He saw the path leading up to the house on Egypt Street. He saw the dusk descending and Abilene running toward him.

7. A   And so it was that Edward took to the road with a tramp and his dog.

Chapters Thirteen & Fourteen

1. A   They traveled on foot. They traveled in empty freight cars. They were always on the move. "But in truth," said Bull, "we are going nowhere. That, my friend, is the irony of our constant movement." Edward rode in Bull's backpack, slung over.

2. D   To his surprise, he began to feel a deep tenderness for the dog.

3. A   During the night, while Bull and Lucy slept, Edward, with his ever-open eyes, stared up at the constellations. He said their names, and then he said the names of the people who loved him. He started with Abilene and then went on to Nellie and Lawrence and from there to Bull and Lucy, and then he ended again with Abilene: Abilene, Nellie, Lawrence, Bull, Lucy, Abilene.

4. C   "Now you have the proper outlaw look," said Bull, standing back to admire his work. "Now you look like a rabbit on the run."

5. B   Soon the men became accustomed to Edward, and word of his existence spread. So it was that when Bull and Lucy arrived at a campfire in another town, another state, another place entirely, the men knew Edward and were glad to see him. "Malone!" they shouted in unison. And Edward felt a warm rush of pleasure at being recognized, at being known.

6. A   After this, wherever Bull and Lucy and Edward went, some tramp would take

Edward aside and whisper the names of his children in Edward's ear.

7. D   "No, sir," said the man again. He looked down at Edward, "No free rides for rabbits." He turned and flung open the door of the carriage, and then he turned back and with one swift kick sent Edward sailing out into the darkness.

Chapters Fifteen & Sixteen

1. D   Pick me up or don't pick me up, the rabbit thought. It makes no difference to me.

2. C   She hung him from a post in her vegetable garden. She nailed his ears to the wooden post and spread his arms out as if he were flying and attached his paws to the post by wrapping pieces of wire around them. In addition to Edward, pie tins hung from the post. They clinked and clanked and shone in the morning sun. "Ain't a doubt in my mind that you can scare them off," the old lady said. Scare who off? Edward wondered. Birds, he soon discovered.

3. B   "Go on, Clyde," said the woman. She clapped her hands. "You got to act ferocious."

Clyde? Edward felt a weariness so intense wash over him that he thought he might actually be able to sigh aloud. Would the world never tire of calling him by the wrong name?

4. A   He saw the stars. But for the first time in his life, he looked at them and felt no comfort. Instead, he felt mocked. You are down there alone, the stars seemed to say to him. And we are up here, in our constellations, together.

5. C   "Bryce," said the old woman. "Git away from that rabbit. I ain't paying you to stand and stare."

6. D   What was it like to have wings? Edward wondered. If he had had wings when he was tossed overboard, he would not have sunk to the bottom of the sea. Instead, he would have flown in the opposite direction, up, into the deep, bright blue sky. And when Lolly took him to the dump, he would have flown out of the rubbish and followed her and landed on her head, holding on with his sharp claws. And on the train, when the man kicked him, Edward would not have fallen to the ground; instead he would have risen up and sat on top of the train and laughed at the man: Caw, caw, caw.

7. A   But when the last nail was out and he fell forward into Bryce's arms, the rabbit felt a rush of relief, and the feeling of relief was followed by one of joy. Perhaps, he thought, it is not too late, after all, for me to be saved.

1. B   "I come to get you for Sarah Ruth," Bryce said. "You don't know Sarah Ruth. She's my sister. She's sick. She had a baby doll made out of china. She loved that baby doll. But he broke it. . . ."

2. D   The house in which Bryce and Sarah Ruth lived was so small and crooked that Edward did not believe, at first, that it was a house. He mistook it, instead, for a chicken coop.

3. B   Never in his life had Edward been cradled like a baby. Abilene had not done it. Nor had Nellie. And most certainly Bull had not. It was a singular sensation to be held so gently and yet so fiercely, to be stared down at with so much love. Edward felt the whole of his china body flood with warmth.

4. C   Bryce said, "You got to look for falling stars. Them are the ones with magic." They were quiet for a long time, all three of them looking up at the sky. Sarah Ruth stopped coughing. Edward thought that maybe she had fallen asleep. "There," she said. And she pointed to a star streaking through the night sky. "Make a wish, honey," Bryce said, his voice high and tight. "That's your star. You make a wish for anything you want."

5. B   The father dropped Edward on the bed, and Bryce picked up the rabbit and handed him to Sarah Ruth. "It don't matter anyway," said the father. "It don't make no difference. None of it."

6. A   Bryce went out to work and Sarah Ruth spent the day in bed, holding Edward in her lap and playing with a box filled with buttons. "Pretty," she said to Edward as she lined up the buttons on the bed and arranged them into different patterns.

7. A   Sarah Ruth opened her eyes. "Dance, Jangles," said Bryce. And then, moving the strings with the sticks with his one hand, Bryce made Edward dance and drop and sway. And the whole while, at the same time, with his other hand, he held on to the harmonica and played a bright and lively tune.

1. B   One month passed and then two and then three. Sarah Ruth got worse. In the fifth month, she refused to eat. And in the sixth month, she began to cough up blood.

2. A   Edward had fallen out of Sarah Ruth's arms the night before and she had not asked for him again. So, face down on the floor, arms over his head, Edward listened as Bryce wept.

3. C   The yelling between the father and son continued, and then there was a terrible moment when the father insisted that Sarah Ruth belonged to him, that she was his girl, his baby, and that he was taking her to be buried. "She ain't yours!" Bryce screamed. "You can't take her. She ain't yours."

4. D   "How many dancing rabbits you seen in your life?" Bryce said to Edward. "I can tell you how many I seen. One. You. That's how you and me are going to make some money. I seen it the last time I was in Memphis. Folks put on any kind of show right there on the street corner and people pay 'em for it. I seen it."

5. A   "Mama," said a small child, "look at that bunny. I want to touch him." He reached out his hand for Edward. "No," said the mother, "dirty." She pulled the child back, away from Edward. "Nasty," she said.

6. D   Bryce started to cry. Edward saw his tears land on the pavement. But the boy did not stop playing his harmonica. He did not make Edward stop dancing.

7. C   An old woman leaning on a cane stepped up close to them. She stared at Edward with deep, dark eyes. Pellegrina? thought the dancing rabbit. She nodded at him. Look at me, he said to her. His arms and legs jerked. Look at me. You got your wish. I have learned how to love. And it's a terrible thing. I'm broken. My heart is broken. Help me.

Chapters Twenty-One & Twenty-Two

1. A   The diner was called Neal's. The word was written in big, red neon letters that flashed on and off. Inside, it was warm and bright and smelled like fried chicken and toast and coffee.

2. B   Go ahead, Marlene, thought Edward. Push me around. Do with me as you will. What does it matter? I am broken. Broken.

3. D   "This is what I think of dancing rabbits," said Neal. And he swung Edward by the feet, swung him so that his head hit the edge of the counter hard. There was a loud crack.

4. C   He was walking on his own, putting one foot in front of the other without any assistance from anybody.

5. D   "You searching for Sarah Ruth?" Bryce asked. Edward nodded. "You got to go outside if you want to see Sarah Ruth," said Bryce. So they all went outside, Lucy and Bull and Nellie and Lawrence and Bryce and Abilene and Edward.

6. A   "Yep," said Lawrence, "that is the Sarah Ruth constellation." He picked Edward

up and put him on his shoulder. "You can see it right there."

7. B   "Malone!" shouted Bull. And with a terrific lunge, he grabbed hold of Edward's feet and pulled him out of the sky and wrestled him to the earth. "You can't go yet," said Bull. "Stay with us," said Abilene. Edward beat his wings, but it was no use. Bull held him firmly to the ground. "Stay with us," repeated Abilene.

Chapters Twenty-Three & Twenty-Four

1. B   "Ah, there you are," the man said. "I can see that you are listening now. Your head was broken. I fixed it. I brought you back from the world of the dead." My heart, thought Edward, my heart is broken.

2. D   He was on a wooden table. He was in a room with sunshine pouring in from high windows. His head, apparently, had been in twenty-one pieces and now was put back together into one. He was not wearing a red suit. In fact, he had no clothes on at all. He was naked again. And he did not have wings.

3. C   "Two options only," he said. "And your friend chose option two. He gave you up so that you could be healed. Extraordinary, really."

4. B   "And then, some day, I will reap the return on my investment in you. All in good time. All in good time. In the doll business, we have a saying: there is real time and there is doll time. You, my fine friend, have entered doll time."

5. A   "Can't I see him?" asked Bryce. He wiped his hand across his nose and the gesture filled Edward with a terrible feeling of love and loss. "I just want to look at him."

6. C   Lucius Clarke sighed. "You may look," he said. "You may look and then you must go and not come back. I cannot have you in my shop every day mooning over what you have lost."

7. A   "You are wondering, perhaps, about your young friend," said Lucius, "the one with the continually running nose. Yes. He brought you here, weeping, begging for my assistance. 'Put him together again,' he said. 'Put him back together.' . . ."

Chapters Twenty-Five & Twenty-Six

1. C   Edward had never cared for dolls. He found them annoying and self-centered, twittery and vain. This opinion was immediately reinforced by his first shelf-mate, a china doll with green glass eyes and red lips and dark brown hair.

2. D   The doll let out a small squeak. "You're in the wrong place," she said. "This is a shop for dolls. Not rabbits." After a long silence, the doll said, "I hope you don't think that anyone is going to buy you." Again, Edward said nothing. "The people who come in here want dolls, not rabbits. They want baby dolls or elegant dolls such as myself, dolls with pretty dresses, dolls with eyes that open and close."

3. A   "I have already been loved," said Edward. "I have been loved by a girl named Abilene. I have been loved by a fisherman and his wife and a tramp and his dog. I have been loved by a boy who played the harmonica and by a girl who died. Don't talk to me about love," he said. "I have known love."

4. B   Day after day, the door to the shop opened and closed, letting in early morning sun or late afternoon light, lifting the hearts of the dolls inside, all of them thinking when the door

swung wide that this time, this time, the person entering the Edward was the lone contrarian. He prided himself on not hoping, on not allowing his heart to lift inside of him. He prided himself on keeping his heart silent, immobile, closed tight.

5. D   In the gloom of the shop, Edward could see that the doll's head, like his, had been broken and repaired. Her face was, in fact, a web of cracks. She was wearing a baby bonnet. . . . "I am old. The doll mender confirmed this. He said as he was mending me that I am at least that. At least one hundred. At least one hundred years old."

6. C   "You disappoint me," said the old doll. Her words made Edward think of Pellegrina: of warthogs and princesses, of listening and love, of spells and curses. What if there was somebody waiting to love him? What if there was somebody whom he would love again? Was it possible?

7. B   Edward's heart stirred. He thought, for the first time in a long time, of the house on Egypt Street and of Abilene winding his watch and then bending toward him and placing it on his left leg, saying: "I will come home to you." No, no, he told himself. Don't believe it. Don't let yourself believe it. But it was too late.

Chapters Twenty-Seven & Coda

1. A   He repeated the old doll's words over and over until they wore a smooth groove of hope in his brain: Someone will come. Someone will come for you.

2. C   The girl smiled and then she stood on her tiptoes and took Edward off the shelf. She cradled him in her arms. She held him in the same ferocious, tender way Sarah

Ruth had held him.

3. A   "Madam," said Lucius Clarke, "could you please attend to your daughter. She is holding a very fragile, very precious, quite expensive doll."

4. B   She put her hand on the locket that hung around her neck. And Edward saw then that it was not a locket at all. It was a watch, a pocket watch. It was his watch.

5. C   Once, there was a rabbit who danced in a garden in springtime with the daughter of the woman who had loved him at the beginning of his journey.

The Miraculous Journey of Edward Tulane

1판 1쇄   2013년 2월 4일
2판 2쇄   2024년 7월 15일

지은이   Kate DiCamillo
기획   이수영
책임편집   김보경 차소향
콘텐츠제작및감수   롱테일 교육 연구소
저작권   명채린
마케팅   두잉글 사업 본부

펴낸이   이수영
펴낸곳   롱테일북스
출판등록   제2015-000191호
주소   04033 서울특별시 마포구 양화로 113, 3층(서교동, 순흥빌딩)
전자메일   help@ltinc.net

ISBN 979-11-91343-90-8 14740